Cities, Economic Inequality and Justice

Increasing economic inequality in cities, and the spatial translation of that into more segregated neighbourhoods, is top of the political agenda in developed countries. While the overall living standards have increased in the last century, the focus has now shifted from poverty to economic differences, with a particular focus on the gap between the very poor and the (ultra-)rich.

The authors observe a common view among policy-makers and researchers alike: that urban-economic inequality and segregation are increasing; that this increase is bad; and that money and people (in the case of segregation) need to be redistributed in response. In six compact chapters, this book enriches and broadens the debate. Chapters bring together the literature on the social effects of economic inequality and segregation and question whether there are sizable effects and what their direction (positive or negative) is. The often conflated concepts of economic inequality (and segregation) and social injustice are disentangled and the moral implications are reflected on.

The book is essential reading for students and academics of Planning Theory, Planning Ethics, Urban Geography, Urban Economics, Economic Geography and Urban Sociology.

Edwin Buitelaar, PhD, is a professor of land and real estate development at Utrecht University and a senior researcher of urban development at the PBL Netherlands Environmental Assessment Agency.

Anet Weterings, PhD, is a senior researcher of regional economic development at the PBL Netherlands Environmental Assessment Agency.

Roderik Ponds, PhD, is a senior researcher at Atlas voor Gemeenten, and a lecturer on Urban Economics at TIAS Business School.

Routledge Focus on Economics and Finance

The fields of economics are constantly expanding and evolving. This growth presents challenges for readers trying to keep up with the latest important insights. Routledge Focus on Economics and Finance presents short books on the latest big topics, linking in with the most cutting-edge economics research.

Individually, each title in the series provides coverage of a key academic topic, whilst collectively the series forms a comprehensive collection across the whole spectrum of economics.

For a full list of titles in this series, please visit https://www.routledge.com/Routledge-Focus-on-Economics-and-Finance/book-series/RFEF

Cities, Economic Inequality and Justice

Reflections and Alternative Perspectives

Edwin Buitelaar, Anet Weterings and Roderik Ponds

Routledge
Taylor & Francis Group

LONDON AND NEW YORK

First published 2018
by Routledge
2 Park Square, Milton Park, Abingdon, Oxon OX14 4RN

and by Routledge
605 Third Avenue, New York, NY 10017

First issued in paperback 2021

Routledge is an imprint of the Taylor & Francis Group, an informa business

Publisher's Note
The publisher has gone to great lengths to ensure the quality of this reprint but points out that some imperfections in the original copies may be apparent.

British Library Cataloguing in Publication Data
A catalogue record for this book is available from the British Library

Library of Congress Cataloging in Publication Data
A catalog record for this book has been requested

ISBN 13: 978-1-03-209662-9 (pbk)
ISBN 13: 978-1-138-28399-2 (hbk)

Typeset in Times New Roman
by diacriTech, Chennai

Contents

Illustrations

Figures

Table

Acknowledgements

The book before you is the latest fruit of a research process that started late 2014, in which urban-economic inequality and segregation in the Netherlands are investigated from both an empirical and a normative angle. It is the follow-up of a Dutch report, *De Verdeelde Triomf* (The Divided Triumph), that all three authors were involved in, two as authors and one as a reviewer. As researchers on the policy-science interface, we wanted to contribute to the policy and the academic debate on this topic in the Netherlands that both, we felt, were often a bit unstructured, prejudiced and alarmist.

Soon we also realised that these qualifications did not apply exclusively to the Netherlands, but that debates in other countries could also benefit from reflections on the causes, the measurement, the normative assessment and the policy implications of urban-economic inequality and segregation. We broadened our scope and explored more international literature and cases from other (developed) countries to be able to live up to our ambition. We hope we succeeded.

Along the way, many people helped us and enriched our thinking. There are some who we want to thank here specifically. We thank our organisations, PBL Netherlands Environmental Assessment Agency and Atlas voor Gemeenten, particularly Ries van der Wouden, Dorien Manting and Gerard Marlet, for giving us the time to work on this book project. Edwin Buitelaar wants to thank professor Stefano Moroni (Politecnico di Milano), in addition, for hosting him in Milan in November 2016 in order to be able to work on his part of the book and for the exchanges on how to improve that. Finally, we want to express our appreciation to Sanne Boschman (Utrecht University) and Barrie Needham (Radboud University Nijmegen) who were kind enough to read the whole book and to make comments about the clarity and coherence of the argument. It goes without saying that the responsibility for the content lies entirely with us, the authors,

Edwin Buitelaar
Anet Weterings
Roderik Ponds

1 Introducing the book

> It is the peculiar and perpetual error of the human understanding to be more moved and excited by affirmatives than negatives.
>
> (Francis Bacon, as cited in Flyvbjerg, 2006, p. 234)

In the late nineteenth and early twentieth centuries, Western cities were magnets for misery, malnutrition and poor hygienic circumstances. Eradicating poverty and improving the living conditions for the working poor was top of the priority list of politicians and planners (Hall, 2014). Anti-urban sentiments were widely present in the utopian urban planning schemes of great twentieth-century designers such as Le Corbusier, Frank Lloyd Wright and Ebenezer Howard (Fishman, 1982). Until the 1980s, large cities such as New York, Chicago and London were in decline. Nowadays, living conditions in developed cities have improved substantially compared to some decades ago. Moreover, cities are not (only) magnets for poverty: they now also attract great wealth and prosperity. There is, so to say, a 'triumph of the city' (Glaeser, 2011). However, not everyone benefits, or at least not to the same extent, as the following quote about London illustrates:

> In this city of contradictions Londoners of different means live utterly separate lives. The wealthiest live in multimillion pound houses, barely using the city's public services, opting for private schools and hospitals. They enjoy one of the finest restaurant and theatre scenes in the world, and live international lives, travelling abroad more frequently than outside the M25. The contrast with the lives of poor Londoners could not be starker. Most of London's poor have jobs, many of which do not pay the minimum wage thanks to unscrupulous companies using tricks like keeping tips to

top up wages. They don't bat an eyelid at commuting over two hours on three buses to get to their office-cleaning jobs because they can't afford the tube, or because they need to start at 4am so they can clear out by the time the office workers arrive. They live with the fear their teenage children will get caught up in the gang violence that barely touches the professionals who walk the same streets in Peckham, Ladbroke Grove and King's Cross. Yes, London has wonderful free museums and parks – but who has time to visit them when you're trying to hold down two or three jobs? ('The Observer View 'on London's Wealth Gap', 2015).

Although the rich and the poor live in the same city, it does not mean they live *with* each other, as the quote above illustrates. In cities, growing socio-economic differences appear to be translated into a growing physical separation of the rich and the poor into different neighbouurhoods. Dutch journalist Arjen van Veelen (2014) illustrates this nicely through the example of the city of St. Louis. He observes two neighbouurhoods separated only by a road (Delmar Boulevard). The northern neighbourhood is quite affluent, while the one to the south is fairly poor (Figure 1.1). Van Veelen frames it as Piketty City, after the bestselling economist.

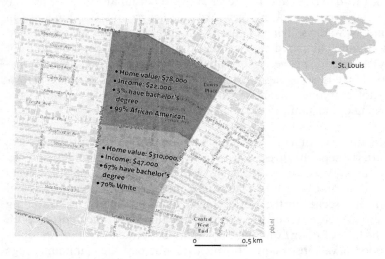

Figure 1.1 Unequal neighbourhoods in St. Louis (Piketty city).
Source: From Van Veelen, A. 2014, August 6.

Thus, in cities, the rich and the poor are assumed to be divided economically and to occupy an almost entirely different spatial life-world, and both divisions appear to intensify. But how do we measure that accurately? What causes economic inequality and segregation in cites? And to what extent is it a societal problem? What are the negative effects of economic inequality in cities, and what is the moral importance of economic equality? Does the spatial separation (i.e. segregation) add to the inequalities that are the result of differences in personal features and circumstances? Alternatively, would it be better if people with significant wealth differences lived immediately next to each other? Would it improve a poor person's wealth or well-being if he or she were to see a cash-rich neighbour plunge into the swimming pool and drive off in a Corvette on a daily basis? These are the kinds of questions that will be addressed in the book before you.

Reflecting on the current debate

The starting point of this book is the common understanding in most advanced economies that (1) urban-economic inequality and the spatial sorting thereof (i.e. segregation) are increasing, (2) that this is a bad thing, and (3) that money and people (in the case of segregation) need to be redistributed in response (e.g., Atkinson, 2015; Dorling 2014; Piketty 2014; Wilkinson & Pickett, 2009). In recent years, many academic contributions have been made to support that view, most of them more generally and not only focused on the urban expression of economic inequality. Among them are some that are incredibly rich in data. Piketty's (2014) bestseller *Capital in the Twenty-First Century* is at the top of that pile. Its impressive historical data analysis demonstrates that economic inequality is increasing in many countries, and that capital differences, rather than income differences, are responsible for that. Another important contributor is the late Tony Atkinson, author of *Inequality – What Can Be Done?* (2015). In this work, he brings together his long-standing methodological and empirical contributions to the issue of inequality. In the area of (economic) segregation, too, the increasing availability of microdata and the progress in econometric techniques have led to a wave of empirical studies that measure segregation, its causes and effects. A recent and fine example is the rich comparative study by Tammaru et al. (2016) in which segregation in 13 European cities is measured and further analysed.

Despite the progress that has been made in empirical descriptions, due to increased, better data and statistical techniques, we believe that the general debate on (urban-) economic inequality and segregation, which sometimes includes the academic contribution to it, needs further advancement in several aspects. In our opinion, it could benefit from (1) more structure and order, (2) from scrutinising taken-for-granted assumptions and measures and (3) from reflecting on the alleged problematic nature of inequality and segregation and the alarmist tone of voice with which this debate is often held. Together, this would improve the discussion and, in turn, that would contribute both to policy effectiveness and political legitimacy as well as to targeting the 'right' societal issue, as we will further explain later in this chapter, and in the rest of the book.

With regard to the first point, it is often unclear what is meant by urban-economic inequality and segregation. There are many forms of urban inequality, and concepts such as (economic) inequality (and its different forms), segregation, poverty and (in)justice are often used interchangeably in the debate while they are 'only' related, and thus not synonymous. We deal with their definitions (see also List of Concepts) and theoretical interconnections.

By the second point we mean that there are many challenges in identifying economic inequality and segregation and interpreting their measures (most notably the Gini coefficient and the dissimilarity index) that do not always receive the attention they deserve. For instance, different inequality statistics lead to different results and conclusions. Not reflecting upon this may result in jumping to the conclusion that inequality or segregation is increasing (or decreasing), while the underlying processes may be more dynamic, complex and counterintuitive than that.

Third and finally, the value judgements about economic inequality (not just urban) and segregation and their foundations are often left implicit, also within the academic literature. Demonstrating that (urban-)economic inequality or segregation is increasing is often deemed enough justification in itself, enough to call for action against it. However, that is a 'normative leap from "is" to "ought"' (Rein & Schön, 1993, p. 148), or, in other words, a jump from empirical descriptions and analyses to specific policy prescriptions and actions. We consider such a jump as being driven by a normative *reflex*, not unlike Pavlov's, rather than by *reflection*. A reflex is an automatic impulse, whereas reflection is a conscious and deliberate attempt to think through the consequences of an observation, opinion or decision. The most prominent and important normative reflex in the inequality debate is the equation of economic inequality to social injustice (which is equated to a need for action) (e.g. Dorling, 2010, p. 13). Sometimes the two are even used interchangeably (e.g. Aghion, Caroli, & García-Peñalosa, 1999, p. 1620).

We will first substantiate and illustrate the presence of normative reflexes by looking at some of the recent influential works before expressing why we believe normative reflections are to be preferred over such reflexes.

One example is Atkinson's *Inequality* (2015), which consists of three parts. The first part describes the development of inequality in both developed and developing countries and the factors that drive it. The other two parts discuss *what* can be done about it in terms of taxation, social security and so on. These two latter parts are not preceded by any discussion of *why* and under which circumstances something should be done.[1] Piketty's *Capital* is quite similar in that respect. From his extensive data analysis, Piketty formulates the policy recommendation that governments should tax capital more heavily than labour (i.e. wages). However, *why* (other than because of the observation that capital differences increase), when and under which circumstances remain unclear. The literature on segregation suffers from the same flaw: bold value judgments and policy prescriptions are often insufficiently backed by normative reflections. For instance, in the earlier mentioned edited volume by Tammaru et al. (2016), the editors occasionally point to the danger of socio-economic segregation as being 'a major challenge threatening the sustainability of urban communities and the competitiveness of European cities' (p. 1) that could 'seriously harm the social stability of our future cities' (pp. 358, 378). However, these claims are neither supported by empirical evidence from either primary sources or the literature, nor along the lines of logic.

We believe there are three main reasons why it is important to have a thorough reflection on government action aimed at reducing economic inequality before choosing to undertake that action (if at all). The first is because we want policies to solve problems. Therefore, it is important to know if and why something is a problem, and why targeting it should be turned into a policy goal, in the first place. Instead of economic inequality or segregation, something else may be at the root of a social or economic problem that economic inequality or segregation is proclaimed to have caused. Targeting these would then be off target. In addition, not every type of inequality or segregation is the same, nor is its impact (see, e.g. de Dominicis, Florax, & de Groot, 2008, p. 660 on the varying degrees of income inequality and the varying impact on economic growth). In that case, different types of inequality and segregation require different forms of action and perhaps different degrees of redistribution (if any) in order to be effective and efficient. The second reason or criterion is legitimacy. Atkinson (2009) himself wrote that justifications for intervention are crucial because, in a democratic country, governments must persuade society of their objectives and actions.

The last reason relates to morality. If a thorough moral reflection leads to the conclusion that economic inequality is not immoral, while reducing it by means of redistributing income is (see, e.g. Nozick, 1974), then it follows logically that, given this moral perspective, a government that redistributes income is acting immorally.[2]

The contribution and the limitations of this book

This book is about economic inequality and segregation in cities. By urban-economic inequality, we mean a skewed wealth and income distribution within the context of a city or city region. This includes wage, income and capital distributions. Urban-economic segregation refers to an uneven distribution of people over the city or city region according to income or wealth. Obviously, there are degrees to which urban-economic inequality and segregation take place: some cities have greater economic inequality and segregation than others.

Cites and city regions are the geographical entities that we choose to look at (i.e. urban-economic inequality), because there the differences between the rich and the poor seem most profound and to increase most substantially (Sassen, 2006). We will focus on urban-*economic* inequality and segregation as the object of our study, not other forms, such as inequality and segregation according to age, gender, race and so on. This does not mean we do not pay attention to these at all. They are relevant as they are linked to or overlap with economic inequality and segregation (Wilkinson & Pickett, 2009, pp. 185–186; Tammaru et al., 2016, p. 365). Therefore, these other inequalities will be touched upon as contextual factors. Another limitation of the scope is that we focus on those issues particular to developed countries. However, although we have developed countries in mind and we use examples from those countries to marshal our arguments, these arguments may well be of use to developing countries.

Why discuss both urban-economic inequality and segregation in one book? We believe it is important to bring together these two social phenomena for two reasons. First, they are *causally* related: no economic inequality, no economic segregation. If there were to be perfect income or wealth equality in a city, there could only be a perfectly even spatial distribution of income or wealth over the city. Economic inequality is thus a *necessary* condition for economic segregation, but not a *sufficient* one. In theory, economic inequality in a city may be evenly distributed over its neighbourhoods. In Chapter 2, we will show that cities with high levels of economic inequality do not necessarily have high levels of economic segregation, and *vice versa*. The way in which and the extent to which economic inequality is turned into economic segregation depends on other factors, such as the welfare system of a country, its housing system, the local housing policy, the local spatial policy and so on (Tammaru et al., 2016).

Second, urban-economic inequality and segregation are *structurally* related, in the sense that they are both intrinsically *relative* concepts. Another term for economic inequality is *relative* poverty, which means that people's economic positions are determined against each other. One person is richer or poorer than another, while, in the case of absolute poverty (see List of Concepts and Chapter 5 in particular), you would say that one is (absolutely) poor and the other rich, regardless of the other person's economic position. Economic *segregation* is also a relative concept as it compares the spatial distribution of a group of people across neighbourhoods with that of another group according to their wealth. A city is segregated if particular wealth groups are over- or underrepresented in one or more neighbourhoods as compared to the presence of other wealth groups. The implication of the notion that both are *relative* concepts is that many empirical-methodological, logical and moral observations apply in a similar way. Therefore, we believe it calls for a joint treatment.

Urban-economic inequality and segregation are not new topics by any means – research topics sometimes seem to come back in cycles. They have a long history, with *Social Justice and the City* by David Harvey (1972) not necessarily functioning as their starting points but at least as one of the early and most influential cornerstones. It still is an important reference in this debate (a revised edition was published in 2009). Other important contributors since are Saskia Sassen (2006), Chris Hamnett (1994, 2003), Enrico Moretti (2012) and Sako Musterd (2002; Musterd & Ostendorf, 1998; Burgers & Musterd, 2002) along with many others. In Chapter 2, we will discuss the literature more extensively.

What, then, is new about these topics? Although urban-economic inequality and segregation are as old as the social construction of cities and go back at least to the ancient Greeks (Glaeser, 2011, p. 69), the subjects recently took centre stage again. This occurred in the slipstream of the more general inequality debate that has been thriving since 2008. The debate was most notably inspired by the publication of Piketty's *Capital in the Twenty-First Century*, although other books that came out just before or after its publication, such as *The Spirit Level* (Wilkinson & Pickett, 2009), *The Price of Inequality* (Stiglitz, 2012), *Inequality and the 1%* (Dorling, 2014) and *Inequality – What Can Be Done?* (Atkinson, 2015), have also been very influential.

Contributing to such topical issues runs the risk of walking down a beaten track. And, indeed, much has already been said. Nevertheless, we believe that some elements remain underemphasised in the mainstream debate, and that there is a demand for bringing together these various elements (theoretical, methodological, empirical, and normative) in an accessible and systematic way.

Our aim is to reflect on the empirical-methodological and normative soundness of the claim that urban-economic inequality and the spatial sorting thereof (i.e. segregation) are increasing, that this is a bad thing and that money and people (in the case of segregation) need to be redistributed in response. Thus, we make a distinction between empirical (i.e. descriptive) and normative (i.e. prescriptive) statements, although we are aware of the fact that the two are strongly related. Regarding inequality, Atkinson states that it 'cannot, in general, be measured without introducing social judgements. Measures such as the Gini coefficient are not purely "statistical" and they embody implicit judgements about the weight to be attached to inequality at different points on the income scale' (Atkinson, 1975, p. 47). Some (constructivist) research traditions therefore reject the distinction between descriptive and prescriptive per se. The argument is often that there are no objects such as facts that exist independent from subjects and their perceptions (e.g. Harvey, 1972, p. 11). However, we think the distinction is possible and necessary. We are fully aware that there is not a world of facts and a world of values: the distinction is not *ontological* but *logical*. It is simply a distinction between types of languages: descriptive (if A happens, then B *will* happen) and prescriptive (A *must* happen, or if A happens, B *must* happen). In responding to the critique that the observer's values guide his descriptions, we quote Chiappero-Martinetti and Moroni:

> This objection does not demonstrate anything *in itself*: in fact, there is no problem in admitting that our values lead us to focus our attention on certain questions rather than others. However, this does not mean that the empirical statements that we will formulate regarding a given phenomenon will not be descriptive and *verifiable as such* by other researchers (2007, p. 364, emphasis in original).

The distinction is also necessary because we must avoid treating empirical observations as a call to action; action should be preceded by explicit normative reflection, as explained earlier (see Section 'Reflecting on the current debate').

In our reflection, we have no intention to reason away the common claim that 'urban- economic inequality and the spatial sorting thereof (i.e. segregation) are increasing, this is a bad thing, and money and people (in the case of segregation) need to be redistributed in response' altogether, but we are convinced that there are some important questions to be asked and, if possible, answered before we can have a meaningful debate and well-considered and balanced policy decisions.[3]

Therefore, we want to disentangle the claim and reflect on the various elements that it is made of. First, we want to reflect on the empirical-methodological side: 'urban-economic inequality and segregation are increasing'. We are not going to argue whether this statement is correct or not: that depends on the country or the region of interest and is therefore a contextual question. In addition, there is now extensive literature showing that economic inequality is increasing in many places in the developed world (e.g. Piketty, 2014; Atkinson, 2015). We do, however, want to discuss the way in which information about economic inequality and segregation is commonly collected, measured and interpreted. There are some important shortcomings when it comes to the most widely used measures for economic inequality (i.e. the Gini coefficient) and segregation (i.e. the dissimilarity index).

Second, we want to reflect on the value judgements, or the normative aspects: to what extent are urban-economic inequality and segregation 'bad' and do they justify policy action? Some argue economic inequality is problematic because it has negative social impacts, on, for instance, health, the economy and social cohesion. But, what do and do we not know about those impacts? There are others who do not (only) look at economic inequality and segregation *instrumentally* (in other words, looking at their impact on other social phenomena), but who argue that they are *intrinsically* bad or, put more academically, unjust (see, e.g. Atkinson, 2015, pp. 11–14 on that distinction). What is the moral relevance of inequality or relative poverty? There is a whole school of thought claiming that absolute poverty is of much greater moral relevance, and that focusing on economic inequality instead may take our attention away from the poor and poverty. We will discuss this based on economic and political philosophy. The final normative reflection we make deals with the adjective *'economic'* (inequality) and the literature's preoccupation with *resource-based* approaches (Nussbaum, 2011, p. 56).

Last but not least, we want this book to have practical relevance. Therefore, we also explore the policy implications of the reflections that we undertake.

We aim for a book that is, on the one hand, scientifically sound and well-embedded in the literature and, on the other, practically relevant for policymakers and (graduate) students. However, in our contradictory ambition to write both a comprehensive and an accessible book, we had to make choices. Accessibility and readability prevailed over completeness. Although we try to cover the most important arguments and counterarguments, the format and length of the book does not allow for an exhaustive literature review and lavish referencing.

It is our ambition to combine empirical-methodological, theoretical and normative insights and to make the book not only analytical and rigorous, but also relevant to policy practice. Because there is not one discipline that covers this theme entirely or sufficiently, the book is interdisciplinary. By combining insights from economics, sociology, geography, planning and philosophy, we believe the book cannot be squeezed into just one disciplinary department of the academic landscape, and we hope that students, scholars and policy-makers alike will be tempted to step out of their comfort zones and enter new or other disciplinary avenues.

We try to illustrate our arguments with practical examples as much as possible. In doing so, there is a bias toward the Netherlands and Dutch cities. We do this not because we believe the Netherlands is representative of all developed countries – Susan Fainstein (2010) considers Amsterdam to be an extreme and almost perfect example of *The Just City*[4] – but because the information about Dutch cities is nearest to hand and because of the great level of detail and good quality of the data. We are convinced that, fundamentally, the empirical–methodological and normative challenges are identical in each country, while the practical and political challenges are obviously contextual and do therefore vary.

Outline

In the remainder of the book, we will subsequently discuss the three parts of the statement we mentioned previously. The first part of the statement 'urban-economic inequality and segregation are increasing'– is discussed in Chapters 2 and 3. Chapter 2 explores theories of how urban-economic inequality and its spatial sorting come about. It links macro processes such as globalisation, demographic changes and technological advancement to the micro level, and individual features and circumstances mediated by urban-economic conditions. Chapter 3 deals with the empirical–methodological questions relating to inequality and segregation: How can we measure them in an appropriate way?

In Chapters 4 and 5, we discuss the second part of the statement—'that this is a bad thing.' In Chapter 4, we do this by exploring urban-economic inequality and segregation *instrumentally*. In other words, by looking at how they impact on *other* social phenomena, such as economic growth, health and social cohesion. Chapter 5 reflects on the relevance of economic inequality and segregation *intrinsically* (i.e. the extent to which they are problematic *in and of themselves*).

In Chapter 6, we draw conclusions based on the previous five chapters and reflect on the last part of the statement: 'money and people (in the case of segregation) need to be redistributed in response.'

Notes

1   In the first section, Atkinson reserves four pages (of over 380 pages) to discuss why economic inequality should be our concern (Atkinson 2015, pp. 11–14), but because he does not go any further than briefly outlining the types of concerns (intrinsic and instrumental concerns; see later), it cannot be counted as a serious start for making a case in favour of reducing economic inequality.
2   To be clear, we are not saying redistribution policies *are* immoral; we are saying that they touch upon issues of morality that need to be reflected upon before proposing action.
3   Neither do we intend to push a 'neoliberal' agenda—as we anticipate some critics may accuse us of—as some do when they do not like the look of an urban study or policy. It is simply a plea for a critical reflection of taken-for-granted ideas and for targeting the 'right' societal problem. According to Hartwitch (2009, p. 23), 'neoliberalism' and its adjective 'neoliberal' have become 'political swearwords.'
4   Uitermark (2011) questions that qualification. According to him, Amsterdam is not a *just* city but just a *nice* city.

References

Aghion, P., Caroli, E., & García-Peñalosa, C. (1999). Inequality and economic growth: The perspective of the new growth theories. *Journal of Economic Literature, 37*(4), 1615–1660.

Atkinson, A. B. (1975). *The Economics of Inequality.* London, UK: Oxford University Press.

Atkinson, A. B. (2009). Economics as a moral science. *Economica, 76*(s1), 791–804.

Atkinson, A. B. (2015). *Inequality – What Can Be Done?* Cambridge, MA: Harvard University Press.

Burgers, J., & Musterd, S. (2002). Understanding urban inequality: A model based on existing theories and an empirical illustration. *International Journal of Urban and Regional Research, 26*(2), 403–413.

Chiappero-Martinetti, E., & Moroni, S. (2007). An analytical framework for conceptualizing poverty and re-examining the capability approach. *The Journal of Socio-Economics, 36*(3), 360–375.

de Dominicis, L., Florax, R. J. G. M., & de Groot, H. L. F. (2008). A meta-analysis on the relationship between income inequality and economic growth. *Scottish Journal of Political Economy, 55*(5), 654–682.

Dorling, D. (2010). *Injustice. Why Social Inequality Persists.* Bristol, UK: The Policy Press.

Dorling, D. (2014). *Inequality and the 1%.* London, UK: Verso.

Fainstein, S. S. (2010). *The Just City*. Ithaca, NY: Cornell University Press.

Fishman, R. (1982). *Urban Utopias in the Twentieth Century: Ebenezer Howard, Frank Lloyd Wright, Le Corbusier.* Cambridge, MA: The MIT Press.

Flyvbjerg, B. (2006). Five misunderstandings about case-study research. *Qualitative Inquiry, 12*(2), 219–245.

Glaeser, E. L. (2011). *The Triumph of the City: How Our Greatest Invention Makes Us Richer, Smarter, Greener, Healthier, and Happier.* New York, NY: Penguin.

Hall, P. (2014). *Cities of Tomorrow: An Intellectual History of Urban Planning and Design Since 1880.* Oxford, UK: Wiley-Blackwell.

Hamnett, C. (1994). Social polarisation in global cities: Theory and evidence. *Urban Studies, 31*(3), 401–425.

Hamnett, C. (2003). *Unequal City: London in the Global Arena.* London, UK: Routledge.

Hartwitch, O. M. (2009). Neoliberalism: The genesis of a political swearword. (CIS Occasional Paper No. 114). Universidad ORT Uruguay, Montevideo, Uruguay, www.ort.edu.uy/facs/boletininternacionales/contenidos/68/neoliberalism68.pdf

Harvey, D. (1972, reprinted in 2009). *Social Justice and the City.* Athens, GA: The University Press.

Moretti, E. (2012). *The New Geography of Jobs.* Boston, MA: Houghton Mifflin Harcourt.

Musterd, S., & Ostendorf, W. (Eds.). (1998). *Urban Segregation and the Welfare State: Inequality and Exclusion.* London, UK: Routledge.

Nozick, R. (1974). *Anarchy, State and Utopia.* New York, NY: Basic Books.

Nussbaum, M. (2011). *Creating Capabilities: The Human Development Approach.* Cambridge, MA: Belknap Press.

Piketty, T. (2014). *Capital in the Twenty-First Century.* Cambridge, MA: Harvard University Press.

Rein, M., & Schön, D. (1993). Reframing policy discourse. In F. Fischer & J. Forester (Eds.), *The Argumentative Turn in Policy Analysis and Planning* (pp. 145–166). London, UK: Duke University Press.

Sassen, S. (2006). *Cities in a World Economy*, (3rd ed.). Thousand Oaks, CA: Pine Forge Press.

Stiglitz, J. E. (2012). *The Price of Inequality: How Today's Divided Society Endangers Our Future.* New York, NY: W. W. Norton & Company.

Tammaru, T., Marcińczak, S., van Ham, M., & Musterd, S. (Eds.). (2016). *Socio-Economic Segregation in European Capital Cities.* London, UK: Routledge.

The Observer View on London's Wealth Gap. (2015). March 8. *The Guardian*, www.theguardian.com/commentisfree/2015/mar/08/observer-view-on-london

Uitermark, J. (2011). An actually existing just city? The fight for the right to the city in Amsterdam. In N. Brenner, P. Marcuse, and M. Mayer (Eds.), *Cities for People, Not for Profit: Critical Urban Theory and the Right to the City* (pp. 197–214). Oxford, UK: Blackwell.

van Veelen, A. (2014). August 6. Welkom in Piketty city. *De Correspondent*, https://decorrespondent.nl/1549/welkom-in-piketty-city/165143708939-e4b3cad9

Wilkinson, R., and Pickett, K. (2009). *The Spirit Level: Why Equality Is Better for Everyone.* London, UK: Penguin Books.

2 Causes of urban-economic inequality and segregation

> Any city, however small, is in fact divided into two, one city of the poor, the other of the rich.
>
> (Plato, as cited in Glaeser, 2011, p. 69)

People differ in many ways – in their talents, personal interests, ambitions and the choices they make in life. These differences naturally lead to differences in individual economic outcomes. People with scarce talents will earn more than those not blessed with such talents.[1] People who work more will have a higher income than equally talented people who choose to work part-time. Risk-taking entrepreneurs may become very wealthy (or very poor) compared to employees. Differences in choices with regard to marriage, children and lifestyle also result in income and wealth differences between between individuals with equal talents and ambitions. In addition, personal 'luck' (whether one is born into a rich or a poor family, for instance) or specific events (e.g. winning the lottery) play a role. Economic inequality is, therefore, something fundamentally inherent to the fact that people are different.

Despite these ever-present inherent differences between people are, and that, in many (Western) countries, economic inequality is firmly lessened by the redistributive effect of taxes and social welfare arrangements (see, e.g. Gornick & Milanovic, 2015), the topic of economic inequality has, once more, become one of the key issues of popular debate. This renewed[2] interest in inequality stems from the broader notion that various structural trends in the economy have deepened the economic inequality in many countries and that this is likely to continue in the future.

Structural trends may have a different impact in different regions and, as a consequence, inequality has a clear geographical dimension within countries. Many countries face an increasing inequality between, on the one hand, rapidly growing (often urban) regions and, on the other, regions and cities that are struggling with economic and population decline (see, e.g. Glaeser, 2011; Moretti, 2012). These increasing differences between regions result in higher levels of economic inequality within countries, but also within successful cities, in which people in both the higher and lower parts of the income distribution are often overrepresented (Sassen, 2006). This increasing economic inequality is often assumed to go hand in hand with an increase in economic segregation in these cities (Musterd & Ostendorf, 1998; Tammaru et al. 2016).

In this chapter, we describe the background of the fundamental trends shaping (urban-)economic inequality and segregation by building on the wide and burgeoning literature on this topic. We do not intend (nor claim) this overview to be exhaustive, as these topics have been studied for many decades in a wide range of scientific disciplines. Rather, this overview is meant to provide a broader picture of the underlying forces that shape the present trends in increasing urban-economic inequality and segregation. This is done in four parts. In the first section, the (global) economic and demographic processes that shape economic inequality in general are described. Next, we focus on the specific position of cities and differences *between* cities and regions with regard to economic inequality, whereas the third section zooms in on inequality *within* cities. The fourth section deals with the causes of the spatial configuration of urban-economic inequality: segregation.

Macro processes and inequality

Many policymakers in Western countries face, or fear to face, an increase in economic inequality. This increase is often attributed to structural changes in the economy. Processes such as technological development, globalisation and deindustrialisation and the rise of the service economy, have affected the employment structure of many (Western) countries in a fundamental way, resulting in larger differences in market incomes. Besides changes in economic structure, developments such as changes in demographic structure or in the system of taxes and social transfers can also lead to increasing economic inequality. We discuss these three possible causes below.

Technological development

Technological development and innovation form an important driver of changes in employment structure (see Katz, 1999; Acemoglu & Autor, 2011 for an extensive overview). New products and services may drive other products or services (or companies, or even entire industries) out of the market. On the one hand, this leads to specific jobs becoming obsolete and, on the other hand, the creation of jobs that no one ever thought of in the past. Of course, this in itself has been the case for centuries. However, many authors argue that the technological developments in the recent past have brought stronger advantages to some groups in society and stronger disadvantages to other groups than they did in the past.

This disparity is most noticeable along the lines of educational level (low-skilled, medium-skilled and high-skilled) and specific skills (non-routine versus routine). New technologies may increase the productivity of people in specific jobs, where technology complements the main tasks of the work involved. These are often jobs that require a high level of education and/or skills that cannot easily be automatised. However, new technology may also be a substitute for the main (manual) tasks of other jobs that often consist of routine tasks that can, to some extent, be automatised. These are typically jobs that require a medium or low level of education. This 'skill-biased technological change' is said to lead to an increase in the number of high-skilled, well-paying jobs with many non-routine tasks and a decrease in the number of middle-class jobs (especially those consisting of routine tasks). In addition, the average income of those with high-skilled jobs is increasing, while that of those with medium- and low-skilled jobs remains constant in many countries, and is even in decline (in terms of purchasing power) in some countries (Stiglitz, 2012, p. 70).[3]

Among others, Autor and Dorn (2013) underline, however, that, besides the growth of high-skilled jobs and the decline of a considerable part of the medium- and low-skilled jobs due to technological changes, the number of low- and medium-skilled jobs in the service industry is actually increasing in many Western countries. Typically, these are jobs that cannot (or at least not easily) be automated. They vary from child-care and nursing jobs to jobs in bars, restaurants and housekeeping. In many countries, an increasing proportion of these jobs are part-time and based on temporal contracts. These jobs lead to an insecure and unstable income (Barbieri, 2009) and are referred to by some as 'precarious jobs' (e.g. Kalleberg, Reskin, & Hudson, 2000).

Some (e.g. Frey & Osborne, 2017) fear that increasing levels of robotisation will even further this process in the future. Others argue that, similar to other innovations in the past, robotisation will also lead to new jobs for both high- and low-skilled people, and that the fear for future robotisation is unnecessary (see, e.g. Brynjolfsson and McAfee, 2014; David, 2015), although, temporarily, adjustment costs may be high for some.

Globalisation

Technological developments have also led to a strong decline in transportation costs. In combination with free-trade arrangements and the increasing ease of international communication (resulting from information and communications technology developments), this has enabled the internationalisation of production value chains. Each step of a production chain (ranging from research and development and marketing to production of parts and assembly) can be located exactly where the circumstance for that part of the production process is best, and this often implies that production is spread across locations in different countries. In combination with the rise of financial globalisation (the increase in foreign direct investment), there is an increase in the international competition for each activity in the value chain. According to many, this competition (in combination with offshoring) has both led to a strong pressure on industrial jobs and wages, especially for the jobs that require a low- or middle-level of education (see, e.g. Autor, Dorn, & Hanson, 2013; Hummels, Jørgensen, Munch, & Xiang, 2014; Wood, 1998). At the same time, higher-educated workers in Western countries are considered to have benefited from these processes due to a higher demand for activities in which Western countries have a comparative advantage. Whereas (in most cases, at least) free trade and internationalisation have a positive effect on the economic growth in countries, this growth is not automatically evenly distributed.

The economic trends described above influence the level and development of economic inequality. Milanovic (2016) and Lakner and Milanovic (2016) analysed the developments of worldwide inequality.[4] From the underlying data and analysis, they conclude that these trends have led to a *decline* of worldwide inequality, mainly due to the rapid growth of (the income of) the middle class in countries such as China and India. At the same time, the income of people at the worldwide top of the income distribution (the top 5 per cent) has undergone a rapid increase as well. The groups that have witnessed no or hardly any growth of income are the lower and middle classes in Western countries and the very poor in underdeveloped countries (mainly in Africa). Milanovic (2016) therefore concludes that processes of skill-based technological change and internationalisation may have simultaneously led to a decline of worldwide inequality and an increase of inequality within countries and continents.

Demographic trends

Besides economic trends, other societal trends, such as changes in demographics, influence inequality as well (see OECD 2011). Many

Western countries face a growth in single-person households, which is both due to a higher share of people who choose not to cohabitate (or not until a later stage in their lives), and to the higher share of elderly people who live on longer after their partner has passed away than they did previously. Many Western countries have also witnessed a rapid increase in educational level and labour participation of women over the last decades (Schwartz, 2010). This has resulted in a rise in double-income households. At the same time, the increasing economic independence of women has also led to an increase in divorces, a trend accompanied by a rise in single-income households with children (often with a relatively low household income). This, in turn, leads to an increase in income inequality at the household level, simply due todue to the income differences between double- and single-income households. On top of that, single-person households are less able to benefit from pooling resources and sharing expenditures than persons in a multi-person households (OECD, 2011).

In addition, people increasingly choose a partner with a similar educational background, leading to what is referred to by Costa and Kahn (2000) as 'power couples': couples consisting of two highly educated, high-income partners. At the same time, people with less education and a lower income tend to choose similar partners as well. Several studies show that these demographic trends have contributed to the rise in income inequality between households (see, e.g. Daly & Valletta, 2006; Peichl, Pestel, & Schneider, 2012).

National institutions

Similar economic and demographic trends may lead to different outcomes in terms of economic inequality across countries. The role of the government is very important in explaining such differences (Stiglitz, 2012). National policies with regard to social security and taxes (progressive or regressive) influence the income distribution directly or indirectly (see, e.g. Fournier & Johansson, 2016). Countries with similar levels of income inequality before taxes and transfers can have very different levels of income inequality in terms of disposable incomes (see also Chapter 3). In addition, the organisation of the education system, labour-market institutions (e.g. minimum wages, role of labour unions), and the housing market influence the level of economic inequality as well (see, e.g. Koeniger, Leonardi, & Nunziata, 2007). The government may also facilitate inequality-enhancing processes of 'rent seeking'– the income one receives from the control of a monopoly – through (hidden) subsidies, laws that make markets less competitive, poor enforcement of competition laws and rules that allow big corporations to take advantage of others (Stiglitz, 2012, pp. 35–64).

Inequality between cities

The impact of international economic trends does not only differ between countries, but also between different cities and regions within a country. David et al. (2013) show, for instance, that the negative impact on jobs and wages from an increase in Chinese imports in the United States differs strongly between local labour markets depending on the relative specialisation in specific industries. Technological changes and internationalisation may lead to growth in some regions but can have a negative impact in other regions, depending on the characteristics of the regional economy and labuor force. The size and share of human capital in cities and regions is by many (e.g. Shapiro, 2006; Glaeser, 2005; Glaeser & Saiz, 2003; Florida, 2002) considered to be key for the capacity of a regional economy to adapt to and profit from these trends. As Moretti (2012, p. 10) states: 'Globalization and technological progress have turned many physical goods into cheap commodities but have raised the economic return on human capital and innovation.'

Economic growth in cities

Human capital and economic growth are increasingly concentrated in (a limited number of) cities and urbanised regions. To some extent, this is of all times and is related to advantages for firms associated with being in close proximity to other firms and households. In the field of economic geography and urban economics, these advantages are referred to as 'agglomeration economies.' The existence of agglomeration economies is the sole reason for the presence of cities in the first place. It is difficult to imagine why someone would want to live in close vicinity to others if there are no advantages attached to that. The advantages for firms that stem from agglomeration economies can be considered a centripetal force attracting firms (and people) to a city. Firms benefit from agglomeration economies due to the presence of a large specialised labor market (labour market pooling), the presence of increased and more specialised suppliers (input sharing) and advantages with regard to the exchange of (informal) knowledge and information (knowledge spillovers) (see Rosenthal & Strange, 2004 for an extensive overview). Firms benefit from labour market pooling due to better matching of demand and supply. It is easier (and less costly) to find the right person for a specific job if there is a large potential labour force. In a similar vein, firms benefit from input sharing in the form of better matching in the suppliers' market, which leads to lower transaction costs. In addition, suppliers are able to specialise in larger markets due to a higher demand, which leads to lower costs and/or a higher quality of the inputs these firms need. Knowledge spillovers refer to the ease of exchange of knowledge and information with other firms, which, in turn, leads to higher levels of innovation. This exchange may be the result of formalised trade relations or collaboration, but they may also be informal, accidental and unintended. In all cases, the importance of face-to-face contacts (see Storper & Venables, 2004) leads to advantages for firms and people, as cities offer the benefits of close proximity and a high density of potential partners (Glaeser & Maré, 2001).

Households enjoy agglomeration economies not only because of a higher supply of potential jobs (labour market pooling), but also because of stronger learning effects, which, in turn, increase their productivity and, ultimately, their wages (see, e.g. de la Roca & Puga, 2017). Moreover, households benefit from a higher supply of consumer services and goods such as bars, restaurants, shops and theatres (see Glaeser, Kolko, & Saiz, 2001 on consumer amenities) and other urban amenities such as historical buildings, resulting from previous concentrations of people in that city (Brueckner, Thisse, & Zenou, 1999). The presence of agglomeration economies offers both households and firms advantages[5] that lead to the growth of cities.

Increasing economic importance of cities

This is, in itself, nothing new. Already in 1890, Marshall (p. 871) stated that 'in almost all countries, there is a constant migration towards the towns. The large towns absorb the very best blood from all the rest, ... the most enterprising, the most highly gifted.' However, in recent decades, cities and urbanised regions became the growth engines of the national economy in many countries. This is the result of the increasing importance of innovative activities and services. As these require higher-educated employees and more face-to-face interactions, the aforementioned agglomeration economies have become increasingly important. These advantages are stronger and more pronounced for higher-educated people and specific industries. Both higher-educated employees and potential partners can be more easily found in cities due to the presence of education centres and a large number of activities in close proximity to one another (Glaeser, 2011). Cities attract talent because there are more education options, better career opportunities, higher wages, a higher supply of consumer amenities (Glaeser et al., 2001), and potential partners (Gautier, Svarer, & Teulings, 2010). The rise of the earlier mentioned power couples has increased demand for strategic locations with good accessibility to a high number of job opportunities even further (Costa & Kahn, 2000). These advantages are stronger and more pronounced for higher-educated people and specific industries.

Not all cities benefit

Cities differ in the presence of research and education centres (e.g. universities), the industry structure, and the supply of amenities and consequently, the share and increase of human capital (see, e.g. Berry & Glaeser, 2005). Agglomeration economies lead to increasing returns to scale for human capital and for human capital-intensive companies in cities. An increase in the number of higher educated people living in a city leads to an increase in the productivity, wages and employment growth in this city, and, as a byproduct, to a growth of inequality between urbanised and less-urbanised regions in many countries. This leads to a situation where some cities and regions face a 'positive spiral,' while those that lack amenities and/or suffer from economic decline due to specific shocks, such as the closure of many plants, face a negative spiral of 'brain drain' and population decline.

As a result, what many countries face is a divergence between 'successful' and 'less successful' cities and regions (see, e.g. Moretti, 2012). Cities and regions that are specialised in industrial activities and routine-based jobs, especially, have a worse starting position in that they face difficulties in economising on the possibilities of the economic trends described in the previous section. Or, as Moretti (2012, p. 14) states:

> a handful of cities with the "right" industries and a solid base of human capital keep attracting good employers and offering high wages, while those at the other extreme, cities with the "wrong" industries and a limited human capital base, are stuck with dead-end jobs and low average wage.

Growing inequalities in cities

Besides increasing inequality between 'successful' and 'less successful' cities, cities (and especially successful cities) face growing economic inequalities within their city boundaries as well. One of the obvious, but nonetheless often neglected, underlying causes is the fact that cities in general have (almost) always had a relatively high share of lower-income, unemployed and homeless people, compared to the less-urbanised parts of a country (see, e.g. Glaeser, Kahn, & Rappaport, 2008a). If (some) cities attract an increasing number of people with a higher education and higher incomes, inequality will rise automatically. This rise is simply the result of the fact that the composition of the population is changing. The opposite holds as well: cities that face a decline in higher educated people (a brain drain) and higher incomes may actually face a decline in inequality (and a decline in average income as well).

On the basis of her Global City research, Saskia Sassen (2006; see Florida & Mellander, 2016, for a similar claim) concludes that the post-industrial, service-oriented (global) city is characterised by growing differences. Her polarisation thesis comes down to claiming that both the top and the bottom of the urban labour market are growing at the expense of the middle class.[6]

Trickle-down effects

It has been argued that the success of cities, particular that of the higher end of the urban labour market trickles down to the lower end, to the poor, Moretti, largely repeating John F. Kennedy, states that 'the rising tide lifts all boats, at least all boats that are in the same city' (Moretti, 2012, p. 63). Conceptually, people with a lower or middle income or education may benefit from the increase in jobs for the higher educated and inhabitants with higher incomes in two ways. First, there may be productivity gains stemming from human-capital externalities. Human-capital externalities may arise if the productivity of a (lower-educated) worker increases by working together in a firm or in the same city with the higher educated, due to the transfer of skills and learning effects (see, e.g. Acemoglu, 1996; Moretti, 2004; Ciccone & Peri, 2006). Ultimately, this will lead to higher productivity and wages for people with a lower or middle income or lower and middle education.

Second, a higher share of people who are higher educated or have a higher income may lead to an increase in the demand for workers with a low level of education (Moretti, 2012). This demand effect may arise in two ways. The first way is by the presence of production complementarities of higher-educated workers (in the place of work) and the second is by consumption effects of higher-income inhabitants (in the place of living). Production complementarities refer to the phenomenon that an increase in the share or the numbers of higher-educated workers may lead to an increase in the demand for workers in jobs that are complementary to the jobs these higher-educated workers fulfil. These jobs are typically found in supporting business services (e.g. security or catering) and often require no or a low level of education (see, e.g. Blien, Südekum, & Wolf, 2006; Südekum, 2008). The consumption effects occur if a higher share or number of the higher educated and higher incomes lead to a higher demand for local consumer services such as restaurants, bars, retail and personal services (e.g. hairdressers, household services) (see Manning, 2004; Mazzolari & Ragusa, 2013). The increase in these jobs, requiring a lower (or medium) educational level, may lead to lower unemployment levels for people with a lower or middle income and education (as shown by Winters, 2013).

Empirical studies (see references above) conclude that these trickle-down effects indeed occur. Moretti (2012) concurs that there are strong multiplier effects when it comes to the presence and growth of jobs in knowledge-intensive fields in innovation-oriented industries in the US. Empirical evidence of these multipliers is found in other countries as well, although the size is typically smaller (see Moretti & Thulin, 2013; PBL, 2016). The rising tide seems to lift boats indeed, or at least some of them.

How does the presence of trickle-down effects influence the size and development of urban inequality? The mere fact that inequality is larger in cities that grow and attract more human capital implies that trickle-down effects are not so big as to lower the level of inequality. The rising tide may lift some boats, but not all boats are lifted equally, let alone that smaller boats are lifted higher than larger boats.

This is, to some extent, caused by the fact that not all jobs (requiring a low- or a middle-level of education) created in bars, restaurants, shops and so on are also fulfilled by people with a low education. The higher educated may (temporarily) accept jobs below their education level, and students may be fulfilling these jobs as a secondary job (see Ponds et al., 2016). So, although jobs that require no or a low level of education are created, the number of low-educated people that actually get these jobs may be a lot smaller.

In a more fundamental way, it is difficult to imagine that the multiplier or trickle-down effect can actually reduce the level of inequality in a city. This would imply that the employment and income growth (for the lower and medium educated) stemming from trickle-down effects were to be stronger than the initial growth of jobs and incomes (for the higher educated), which created these trickle-down effects in the first place.

Although trickle-down effects do lead to the benefits of an increase in human capital for all inhabitants in a city, both factors make it unlikely that trickle down effects lead to a lower level of inequality. However, it is important to note that, without these effects, inequality would be (even) greater since fewer jobs would be available to those with a lower (or medium) education.

Housing market dynamics

Another important factor influencing the level of inequality in cities is the housing market. In popular cities that attract human capital, the demand for housing goes up. As it is difficult to increase the supply of housing in the short run (the process of planning and building takes time) and, in many cities, also in the long run (for instance, due to zoning and planning restrictions), this leads to higher prices (see, e.g. Glaeser, Gyourko, & Saks, 2005; Glaeser, Gyourko, & Saiz, 2008b; Hilber & Vermeulen, 2016).

In cities with high and increasing house prices, a high income or a double income (at the household level) may be necessary to afford renting or buying a house that matches one's needs. People with low- or medium-level incomes may find it increasingly difficult to find a house they can afford. People with a low income will be increasingly dependent upon the supply of social or public housing. The availability of social housing differs between countries and cities but, in popular cities, demand typically exceeds supply, and some people with lower incomes are more or less 'forced' to move out of the city if they want a new or bigger house. Middle incomes run the risk of being squeezed out: they are not eligible for social housing but lack the financial means to buy or rent in the private sector. This may result in a decline in the number and share of lower and middle incomes in cities as they move out to nearby (suburban) towns (Cooke & Denton, 2015; Hochstenbach & Musterd, 2017). This, in turn, may increase the level of inequality in cities – simply because only the low incomes (through social housing) and high incomes can find a house in these cities. In this way, even without the actual income levels of people changing, changes in house prices and in the housing provision, and the selective in- and out-migration that follows from that, may lead to increasing inequality in cities.

This process may be furthered by real estate development and investment. Developers and investors are likely to add relatively expensive houses (aiming for higher incomes) to the existing housing stock as prices of land will be high in these cities.

The increase in prices also adds to inequality in cities in another way. As the value of houses goes up, owners benefit from capital gains, whereas renters will be faced with increasing rents. This leads to increasing wealth differences between owners and renters in cities.

Economic segregation in cities

Economic inequality and economic segregation often go hand in hand. People with different levels of income and wealth hardly ever live randomly spread across a city – they are typically concentrated within specific neighborhoods. Residential segregation is the degree to which two or more groups live separately from one another, in different parts of the urban fabric (Massey & Denton, 1988, p. 282).

Economic inequality and economic segregation are related but not the same (see Chapter 1 and the List of Concepts). The distinction is relevant and exceeds semantics, since not separating them might eventually lead to targeting the 'wrong' social problem. For instance, policies targeting high levels of economic segregation are often indirectly and implicitly based on the political aim of lowering inequality (see, for instance, Chapter 6). But the indirectness makes them unlikely to be effective and efficient.

Economic inequality is a necessary condition for economic segregation but not sufficient. There are also other factors at play. Residential preferences and opportunities of people affect the way segregation comes about and changes. Those are discussed in the remainder of this section.

Causes of economic segregation

Economic segregation results, in the first place, from differences in the popularity of neighbourhoods and in individual (financial) opportunities. The differences in popularity reflect a difference in the 'quality of life' that a neighbourhood supplies. This quality of life encompasses different types of amenities (e.g. parks, historical buildings, water, bars and restaurants), lower crime rates and better accessibility (e.g. distance to a major train station or travel times to the main economic centres) and so on. Prices are higher for these areas due to a higher demand compared to that of other, less popular, areas. This leads to a concentration of people who can afford to live in the 'best' areas of a city. Consequently, a more segregated city is typically characterised by the fact that more affluent people enjoy a better 'quality of life' in their neighbourhoods than less affluent people in theirs because the former can afford the higher prices.

Besides differences in (financial) opportunities, differences in residential preferences may also lead to economic segregation. As 'birds of a feather flock together,' people with similar (socio-)economic characteristics tend to live in the same neighbourhoods. However, segregation by economic characteristics often coincides with residential preferences.

For instance, families with two working parents and children tend to have a higher household income than young people in their twenties who have just finished their education. At the same time, families tend to favour child-friendly neighbourhoods with houses with multiple rooms, whereas recently graduated single people in their twenties may favour neighbourhoods with a bustling nightlife. These differences in residential preferences may lead to a segregation of these two types of households, but, at the same time, also to segregation by income due to their differences in income and wealth. This issue of observational equivalence makes it difficult to determine whether economic segregation is driven by differences in (financial) opportunities or by differences in preferences. Especially since, in most cities, both of these processes occur simultaneously. In addition to this, people with similar incomes may prefer to live in the vicinity of each other if they value a low level of income inequality in their neighbourhood (see Luttmer, 2005; Chapter 4).

Finally, the characteristics of the housing market in a city influence the level of economic segregation. Two identical cities with a similar level of inequality may face a very different level of segregation depending on, among other things, how the different types of houses are located within the city. In (almost) all cities, houses in the same neighbourhoods share some similarity, as these are often built in blocks during the same period. Some neighbourhoods may consist of detached or semidetached houses built in a specific construction period with a high housing quality, whereas other neighbourhoods consist of large-scale apartment buildings from another construction period with relatively poor quality.

In addition to these differences in physical structure, there are differences in the ownership structure. Some neighbourhoods may be dominated by owner-occupied houses, whereas other neighbourhoods may consist mainly of private or social rental homes. In cities where social housing is concentrated in a few neighbourhoods, economic segregation will, *ceteris paribus*, be higher than in cities where social housing is more evenly distributed across all neighbourhoods. Whether the first is to be preferred over the latter is a topic we will touch upon in Chapters 4 and 5.

What causes changes in the level of economic segregation?

The level of economic segregation may increase (or decrease) over time in cities for various reasons. Most attention in the literature has been given to selective mobility and migration. If people who move in or out a neighbourhood differ in income and wealth from those in the rest of the neighbourhood, the composition of the neighbourhood (in economic terms) changes, which could lead to a higher or lower level of segregation of the city as a whole. Selective migration may be the result of changes in individual preferences for housing and neighbourhoods as people grow older and their household situation (having a partner or a family) and income changes (see Rossi, 1955; Mulder, 1993). These individual changes may lead to specific household types moving in and out of specific neighbourhoods, depending on the characteristics of both the neighbourhood and the housing stock. Besides changes in individual preferences, changes in neighbourhood characteristics (including the housing stock) may lead to selective migration as well. Negative developments, such as an increase in crime, may lead to an outflow of those people who can afford an alternative, which, in turn, could also lead to an increase of economic segregation.

Real estate developments, such as the construction of new houses in some areas of a city or the restructuring of neighbourhoods, may trigger a selective in- or outflow of people to or from some neighbourhoods as well (see, e.g. South and Crowder, 1997; van Dam et al., 2010). If large expensive houses are added to neighbourhoods where many people with lower incomes live, it could lead to less segregation. If new, suburban neighbourhoods with many owner-occupier dwellings are added to a city, families with higher incomes may leave existing neighbourhoods, which may very well lead to an increase in economic segregation.

Whereas real estate developments change the supply side of the housing market, many popular cities face a change in economic segregation due to demand factors.[7] An increase in demand stemming from higher incomes, or the higher educated moving to a city, may lead to gentrification (see Hochstenbach, 2017 for a recent study for the Netherlands). Gentrification refers to the process of economic 'upgrading' of relatively poor neighbourhoods, primarily through the inflow of people with more wealth than the existing and previous neighbourhood population. Gentrification may lead to a situation where, in some neighbourhoods, people with lower incomes are less likely to be able to afford living there than they did before. If this is furthered by supply side factors such as urban restructuring, privatization of social housing, or new real estate development aiming at higher incomes, many argue that gentrification is, basically, pushing poor people out of 'their' neighbourhoods, leading to household displacement and even community conflicts (Atkinson, 2004). Others (e.g. Freeman, 2006) are less negative and argue that there are both positive and negative effects on the people with lower incomes living in gentrifying neighbourhoods (see also Chapter 4). Gentrification may initially lower the level of economic segregation, but, over time, it may lead to higher levels of economic segregation, depending on how the composition of a gentrifying neighbourhood, and the other neighbourhoods in a city, change (Tammaru et al., 2016).

Although selective migration is an important driver of economic segregation, even without anyone moving in or out their neighbourhoods, 'in situ' change may lead to higher or lower levels of segregation in cities (Bailey, 2012; Jivraj, 2013). In situ change, in relation to economic segregation, refers to the changes in income and wealth of people of people in a neighbourhood that will lead to changes in the level of economic segregation without anyone moving in or out. Neighbourhoods may, for instance, change from high-income to lower- or middle-income neighbourhoods if a large part of the population retires from working. Other neighbourhoods may be hit harder than others in times of economic crisis, for instance, because workers of plants live close together in specific neighbourhoods.

Altogether, it is clear that the level and development of economic segregation are influenced by a large number of factors, touched upon in the sections above. These factors are shaped by both national and local institutions (national housing systems, local urban planning regimes and so on). Consequently, cities that face an increase of economic inequality at the city level due to the inflow of higher-educated people and higher incomes, do not necessarily experience an (equal) increase in economic segregation as well (Tammaru et al., 2016).

Notes

1   This is the 'marginal production theory': 'if someone has a scarce and valuable skill, the market will reward him amply, because of his greater contribution to output' (Stiglitz 2012, p. 37).
2   The topic of inequality has, of course, always been studied in economics and among other scientific fields, ranging from Karl Marx in the nineteenth century to Kuznets in the fifties of the previous century.
3   Whereas the demand for higher-educated workers may have risen due to technological developments, the supply (the size and share) of the higher-educated labour force has increased in most countries as well. However, the fact that wages are typically increasing at a stronger rate for higher educated people implies that demand has grown stronger than supply (see Goldin & Katz 2009 for a broader discussion on this).
4   They presented the famous elephant graph. In this graph, the worldwide population is divided into income percentiles on the horizontal axis (ranging from lowest income on the left to highest income on the right). The vertical axis shows the change in real income between 1998 and 2008. The line connecting all data points has the shape of an elephant: a very low increase in real income for the lowest deciles, a high increase for the deciles up to the sixth and seventh deciles, and a high increase for the highest deciles.

5 Note that agglomeration disadvantages such as higher prices for houses, traffic jams and higher levels of crime and pollution are present as well. These may function as a counterforce to agglomeration advantages and, at least conceptually, to an optimal city size: a city where the net marginal effect of the sum of agglomeration advantages and disadvantages of additional growth is zero.

6 Hamnett (1994) has questioned the polarisation thesis and proposed an alternative: the professionalisation thesis. He argues that the transition from an industrial city to a city in which the service economy is dominant does not have a polarising effect, but leads, as a result of better education, to an increasing middle class and a decreasing lower class.

7 In practice, supply and demand influence each other.

References

Acemoglu, D. (1996). A microfoundation for social increasing returns in human capital accumulation. *The Quarterly Journal of Economics, 111*(3), 779–804.

Acemoglu, D., & Autor, D. (2011). Skills, tasks and technologies: Implications for employment and earnings. In O. Ashenfelter & D. E. Card (Eds.), *Handbook of Labor Economics* (Vol. 4B, pp. 1043–1171). Amsterdam, the Netherlands: Elsevier.

Atkinson, R. (2004). The evidence on the impact of gentrification: New lessons for the urban renaissance? *European Journal of Housing Policy, 4*(1), 107–131.

Autor, D. H., & Dorn, D. (2013). Inequality and specialization: The growth of low-skill service jobs in the United States. *American Economic Review, 103*(5), 1553–1597.

Autor, D. H., Dorn, D., & Hanson, G. H. (2013). The China syndrome: Local labor market effects of import competition in the United States. *The American Economic Review, 103*(6), 2121–2168.

Bailey, N. (2012). How spatial segregation changes over time: Sorting out the sorting processes. *Environment and Planning A, 44*, 705–722.

Barbieri, P. (2009). Flexible employment and inequality in Europe. *European Sociological Review, 25*(6), 621–628.

Berry, C. R., & Glaeser, E. L. (2005). The divergence of human capital levels across cities. *Papers in Regional Science, 84*(3), 407–444.

Blien, U., Südekum, J., & Wolf, K. (2006). Local employment growth in West Germany: A dynamic panel approach. *Labour Economics, 13*(4), 445–458.

Brueckner, J. K., Thisse, J. F., & Zenou, Y. (1999). Why is central Paris rich and Detroit poor? An amenity based theory. *European Economic Review, 43*(1), 91–107.

Brynjolfsson, E., & McAfee, A. (2014). *The Second Machine Age: Work, Progress, and Prosperity in a Time of Brilliant Technologies*. New York, NY: W. W. Norton & Company.

Ciccone, A., & Peri, G. (2006). Identifying human-capital externalities: Theory with applications. *Review of Economic Studies, 73*(2), 381–412.

Cooke, T. J., & Denton, C. (2015). The suburbanization of poverty? An alternative perspective. *Urban Geography, 36*(2), 300–313.

Costa, D. L., & Kahn, M. E. (2000). Power couples: Changes in the locational choice of the college educated, 1940–1990. *The Quarterly Journal of Economics, 115*(4), 1287–1315.

Daly, M., & Valletta, R. (2006). Inequality and poverty in the United States: The effects of rising dispersion of men's earnings and changing family behaviour. *Economica, 73*(289), 75–79.

David, H. (2015). Why are there still so many jobs? The history and future of workplace automation. *The Journal of Economic Perspectives, 29*(3), 3–30.

David, H., Dorn, D. & Hanson, G. H. (2013). The China syndrome: Local labor market effects of import competition in the United States. *The American Economic Review, 103*(6), 2121–2168.

de la Roca, J., & Puga, D. (2017). Learning by working in big cities. *The Review of Economic Studies, 84*(1), 106–142.

Florida, R. (2002). *The Rise of the Creative Class: And How It Is Transforming Work, Leisure, Community and Everyday Life.* New York, NY: Basic Books.

Florida, R., & Mellander, C. (2016). The geography of inequality: Difference and determinants of wage and income inequality across US metros. *Regional Studies, 50*(1), 79–92.

Fournier, J. M., & Johansson, Å. (2016). *The Effect of the Size and the Mix of Public Spending on Growth and Inequality.* Paris, France: OECD.

Freeman, L. (2006). *There Goes the 'Hood: Views of Gentrification from the Ground Up.* Philadelphia, PA: Temple University Press.

Frey, C. B., & Osborne, M. A. (2017). The future of employment: How susceptible are jobs to computerisation? *Technological Forecasting and Social Change, 114*(1), 254–280.

Gautier, P. A., Svarer, M., & Teulings, C. N. (2010). Marriage and the city: Search frictions and sorting of singles. *Journal of Urban Economics, 67*(2), 206–218.

Glaeser, E. L. (2005). Reinventing Boston: 1630–2003. *Journal of Economic Geography, 5*(2), 119–153.

Glaeser, E. L. (2011). *The Triumph of the City. How Our Greatest Invention Makes Us Richer, Smarter, Greener, Healthier, and Happier.* New York, NY: Penguin.

Glaeser, E. L., and Maré, D. C. (2001). Cities and skills. *Journal of Labor Economics, 19*(2), 316–342.

Glaeser, E. L., and Saiz, A. (2003). *The Rise of the Skilled City.* Cambridge, MA: National Bureau of Economic Research.

Glaeser, E. L., Kolko, J., and Saiz, A. (2001). Consumer city. *Journal of Economic Geography, 1*(1), 27–50.

Glaeser, E. L., Gyourko, J., and Saks, R. (2005). Why is Manhattan so expensive? Regulation and the rise in house prices. *Journal of Law and Economics, 48*(2), 331–370.

Glaeser, E. L., Kahn, M. E., and Rappaport, J. (2008a). Why do the poor live in cities? The role of public transportation. *Journal of Urban Economics, 63*(1), 1–24.

Glaeser, E. L., Gyourko, J., & Saiz, A. (2008b). Housing supply and housing bubbles. *Journal of Urban Economics, 64*(2), 198–217.

Goldin, C. D., & Katz, L. F. (2009). *The Race between Education and Technology*. Cambridge, MA: Harvard University Press.

Gornick, J., & Milanovic, B. (2015, May). Income inequality in the United States in cross-national perspective: Redistribution revisited (. Luxembourg Income Study Center Research Brief No.1). Luxembourg Income Study Center at the Graduate Center, City University of New York, www.gc.cuny.edu/CUNY_GC/media/CUNY-Graduate-Center/PDF/Centers/LIS/LIS-Center-Research-Brief-1-2015.pdf

Hamnett, C. (1994). Social polarisation in global cities: Theory and evidence. *Urban Studies, 31*(3), 401–425.

Hilber, C. A., & Vermeulen, W. (2016). The impact of supply constraints on house prices in England. *The Economic Journal, 126*(591), 358–405.

Hochstenbach, C. (2017). Inequality in the gentrifying European city. (Unpublished doctoral dissertation). Amsterdam, the Netherlands: University of Amsterdam.

Hochstenbach, C., & Musterd, S. (2017). Gentrification and the suburbanization of poverty: Changing urban geographies through boom and bust periods. Urban Geography, 1–28, doi: 10.1080/02723638.2016.1276718

Hummels, D., Jørgensen, R., Munch, J., & Xiang, C. (2014). The wage effects of offshoring: Evidence from Danish matched worker-firm data. *The American Economic Review, 104*(6), 1597–1629.

Jivraj, S. (2013). The components of socioeconomic neighbourhood change: An analysis of school census data at varying spatial scales in England. In M. van Ham, D. Manley, N. Bailey, L. Simpson, & D. Maclennan (Eds.), *Understanding Neighbourhood Dynamics* (pp. 183–201). Dordrecht, the Netherlands: Springer.

Kalleberg, A. L., Reskin, B. F., & Hudson, K. (2000). Bad jobs in America: Standard and nonstandard employment relations and job quality in the United States. *American Sociological Review, 65*(2), 256–278.

Katz, L. F. (1999). Changes in the wage structure and earnings inequality. In O. Ashenfelter & D. E. Card (Eds.), *Handbook of Labor Economics* (Vol. 3A, pp. 1463–1555). Amsterdam, the Netherlands: Elsevier.

Koeniger, W., Leonardi, M., & Nunziata, L. (2007). Labor market institutions and wage inequality. *Industrial and Labour Relations Review, 60*(3), 340–356.

Lakner, C., & Milanovic, B. (2016). Global income distribution: From the fall of the Berlin Wall to the Great Recession. *World Bank Economic Review, 11*(2), 203–232.

Luttmer, E. F. P. (2005). Neighbors as negatives: Relative earnings and well-being. *Quarterly Journal of Economics, 120*(3), pp. 963–1002.

Manning, A. (2004). We can work it out: The impact of technological change on the demand for low-skill workers. *Scottish Journal of Political Economy, 51*(5), 581–608.

Marshall, A. (1890). *Principles of Economics: An Introductory Volume* (8th ed.). London, UK: Macmillan.

Massey, D. S., & Denton, N. A. (1988). The dimensions of residential segregation. *Social Forces, 67*(2), 281–315.

Mazzolari, F., & Ragusa, G. (2013). Spillovers from high-skill consumption to low-skill labor markets. *The Review of Economics and Statistics, 95*(1), 74–86.

Milanovic, B. (2016). *Global Inequality: A New Approach for the Age of Globalization*. Cambridge, MA: Harvard University Press.

Moretti, E. (2004). Human capital externalities in cities. In V. Henderson & J. F. Thisse (Eds.), *Handbook of Urban and Regional Economics* (Vol. 4, pp. 2243–2291). Amsterdam, the Netherlands: Elsevier.

Moretti, E. (2012). *The New Geography of Jobs*. Boston, MA: Houghton Mifflin Harcourt.

Moretti, E., & Thulin, P. (2013). Local multipliers and human capital in the United States and Sweden. *Industrial and Corporate Change, 22*(1), 339–362.

Mulder, C. H. (1993). *Migration Dynamics: A Life Course Approach*. Amsterdam: Thesis Publishers.

Musterd, S., & Ostendorf, W. (1998). *Urban Segregation and the Welfare State: Inequality and Exclusion in Western Cities*. Oxford, UK: Routledge.

OECD. (2011). *Growing Income Inequality in OECD Countries: What Drives It and How Can Policy Tackle It?* Paris, France: OECD.

PBL (2016). *De Verdeelde Triomf* [The Divided Triumph]. Den Haag, the Netherlands: Planbureau voor de Leefomgeving.

Peichl, A., Pestel, N., & Schneider, H. (2012). Does size matter? The impact of changes in household structure on income distribution in Germany. *Review of Income and Wealth, 58*(1), 118–141.

Ponds, R., Marlet, G., van Woerkens, C., & Garretsen, H. (2016). Taxi drivers with a PhD: Trickle down or crowding-out for lower educated workers in Dutch cities? *Cambridge Journal of Regions, Economy and Society, 9*(2), 405–422.

Rosenthal, S. S., & Strange, W. C. (2004). Evidence on the nature and sources of agglomeration economies. In V. Henderson & J. F. Thisse (Eds.), *Handbook of Urban and Regional Economics* (Vol. 4, pp. 2119–2171). Amsterdam, the Netherlands: Elsevier.

Rossi, P. H. (1955). *Why Families Move: A Study in the Social Psychology of Urban Residential Mobility*. Glencoe, IL: Free Press.

Sassen, S. (2006). *Cities in a World Economy* (3rd ed.). Thousand Oaks, CA: Pine Forge Press.

Schwartz, C. R. (2010). Earnings inequality and the changing association between spouses' earnings. *American Journal of Sociology, 115*(5), 1524–1557.

Shapiro, J. M. (2006). Smart cities: Quality of life, productivity, and the growth effects of human capital. *The Review of Economics and Statistics, 88*(2), 324–335.

South, S. J., & Crowder, K. D. (1997). Residential mobility between cities and suburbs: Race, suburbanization, and back-to-the-city moves. *Demography, 34*(4), 525–538.

Stiglitz, J. E. (2012). *The Price of Inequality: How Today's Divided Society Endangers our Future*. New York, NY: W. W. Norton & Company.

Storper, M., & Venables, A. (2004). Buzz: Face-to-face contact and the urban economy. *Journal of Economic Geography, 44*), 351–370.

Südekum, J. (2008). Convergence of the skill composition across German regions. *Regional Science and Urban Economics, 38*(2), 148–159.

Tammaru, T., Marcińczak, S., van Ham, M., & Musterd, S. (Eds.). (2016). *Socio-Economic Segregation in European Capital Cities*. London, UK: Routledge.

van Dam, F., Boschman, S., Peeters, P., van Kempen, R., Bolt, G., & Ekamper, P. (2010). *Nieuwbouw, Verhuizingen en Segregatie: Effecten van Nieuwbouw op de Bevolkingssamenstelling van Stadswijken* [New development, relocations and segregation. Effects on neighbourhood composition.]. The Hague, the Netherlands: Planbureau voor de Leefomgeving.

Winters, J. V. (2013). Human capital externalities and employment differences across metropolitan areas of the USA. *Journal of Economic Geography, 13*(5), 799–822.

Wood, A. (1998). Globalisation and the rise in labour market inequalities. *The Economic Journal, 108*(450), 1463–1482.

3 Reflecting on the measurement

[Inequality] cannot, in general, be measured without introducing social judgements. Measures such as the Gini coefficient are not purely 'statistical' and they embody implicit judgements about the weight to be attached to inequality at different points on the income scale.

(Atkinson, 1975, p. 47)

Empirical measurement is key to obtaining a better understanding of the extent and the development direction of inequality and its spatial sorting. However, many methodological decisions need to be made before accurate statistics can be provided. Paying insufficient attention to the challenges and problems in measuring inequality and segregation and the interpretation of these measures can result in jumping to conclusions about changes in inequality or segregation, while the actual situation may be more complex and counterintuitive.

In this chapter, we are not going to debate whether the often-heard statement that inequality and segregation are increasing is correct or not: that depends on the country, region or city of interest, and is, as such, a contextual question. We do discuss the way in which information about inequality and segregation is commonly collected, measured and interpreted. As such, we demonstrate how the most common ways of measuring inequality and segregation (the Gini coefficient and the dissimilarity index, respectively, when applied to income levels) sketch only part of the picture.

Measuring inequality and segregation asks for a reflection on *how* to measure, but also of *what* to measure. We start with discussing the *how* question, by illustrating the different considerations through the most used indicator of economic inequality and segregation: income. Next, we focus on the *what* question and discuss the use of income as an indicator of standard of living. Finally, we explain the difference between inequality and income mobility (and segregation and residential mobility likewise). Inequality and segregation only provide static snapshots of the distribution of income or people, while income and residential mobility sketch a dynamic picture of the changes that people experience in income position and residential location.

How to measure inequality

Economic inequality refers to the skewness of the distribution of an economic indicator, often of income. Thus, it provides information on the extent to which some people in the city have a different income than others. Measures of income inequality only provide information about income *differences* among the population of a city and not into income *levels*. Inequality is not the same as (absolute) poverty (see Chapter 5; List of Concepts).

The Gini coefficient

By far, the most common way to measure inequality is the Gini coefficient (de Maio, 2007). To calculate the Gini coefficient, each person in the population is placed in ascending order, with the person with the lowest income first and the person with the highest income last. Using that information, the Lorenz curve can be plotted (see Figure 3.1): the cumulative distribution of income (y-axis) against the associated cumulative share of the relevant population (x-axis). This curve shows which share of the population earns which share of the total income. In case of perfect equality, the Lorenz curve is equal to the diagonal. The more the

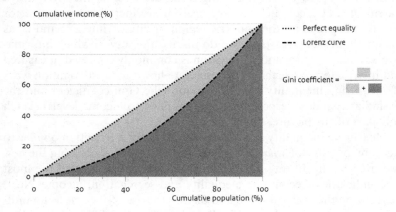

Figure 3.1 Calculating the Gini coefficient.

Lorenz curve of a city deviates from the diagonal, the higher the income inequality. The Gini coefficient measures this deviation and is equivalent to the size of the area between the Lorenz curve and the diagonal divided by the total area under the diagonal (see Appendix for the formula).

An important reason why the Gini coefficient is such a popular statistic is that it is context, scale and population independent. Interpreting the Gini coefficient for a certain city does not require any information about the inequality of previous years or in other cities. A single Gini coefficient already provides a lot of information about the inequality in a city, because the value of the Gini coefficient always varies between 0 and 1. A value of 0 indicates that each person has the same income (i.e. complete equality), while 1 implies that all the income of a country or city is owned by a single person (i.e. complete inequality). Furthermore, the values of the Gini coefficient can easily be compared across countries or cities, as the Gini coefficient is context-independent.[1] This is why organisations, such as the Organisation for Economic Co-operation and Development (OECD) and the World Bank, often use Gini coefficients to compare the developments in income inequality of different countries or cities over time (e.g. OECD, 2011; World Bank, 2016).[2]

Limits to the scope

The Gini coefficient is incapable of differentiating between different kinds of inequalities (de Maio, 2007). Cities with the same total income but very different income distributions can have the same Gini coefficient, as Figure 3.2 illustrates for two fictive cities, each with ten inhabitants.

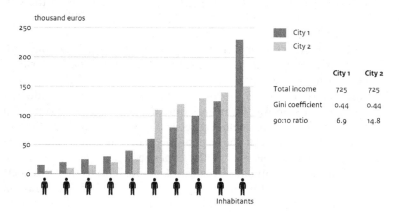

Figure 3.2 Income distribution of two fictive cities.

Furthermore, the Gini coefficient is oversensitive to changes in the middle of the distribution compared to changes at the top and the bottom (Allison, 1978). Consequently, studies of income inequality using the Gini coefficient tend to overlook developments at the extremes (Salverda, 2011). This is an important limitation, because the political debate on income inequality often focuses on developments at either end of the income distribution. Think, for instance, about the heated debate in the United States (and elsewhere) about the increasing amount of income that is earned by the top 1 per cent (e.g. Dorling, 2014).

While the Gini coefficient provides useful information about income inequality, it is important to understand that it is neither the sole, nor necessarily the most appropriate, measure (de Maio, 2007). A good understanding of how income inequality is developing asks for complementing the Gini coefficient with other measures of inequality, with the ratio (or distribution) statistics and Theil's T index being the ones used most often.

Ratio statistics provide additional information about the difference between the extremes of the income distribution (e.g., Salverda & Atkinson, 2007). An often-used example is the P90:P10 percentile ratio. To obtain this statistic, the upper bound value of the ninth decile (10 per cent of people with the highest income) is divided by that of the first, and lowest, decile (10 per cent of people with the lowest income). Besides the bound values of deciles, any other distribution statistic can be used, focusing, for instance, on differences between the bottom and the middle (P50:P10 ratio) or when interested in the position of the top 1 per cent (P99:P90 ratio).[3]

The example in Figure 3.2 illustrates how the Gini coefficient and the P90:P10 ratios give a different picture of the inequality in the two fictive cities. While the Gini coefficient is the same, the P90:P10 ratios emphasise the large differences between the incomes at the top and the bottom of both distributions: in city 1, the 10 per cent of people with the highest income earn almost seven times more than the 10 per cent with the lowest incomes and, in city 2, this difference is even greater (15 times). But, contrary to the Gini coefficient, ratio statistics do not measure inequality among the entire population: information is limited to those who belong to the included deciles or percentiles. Therefore, to obtain a complete picture of the level of inequality, it is best to combine these statistics with the insights of the Gini coefficient.

Theil's T index is a popular alternative (or addition) to the Gini coefficient, because it allows for measuring the extent to which inequality in the total population can be attributed to income differences between subgroups (Shorrocks, 1980). Contrary to the Gini coefficient, this statistic is fully decomposable.[4] Consequently, the level of inequality can be broken down by population groups, income sources or other dimensions (World Bank, 2005). This enables researchers to address questions such as whether inequality in the UK largely follows from differences between London and the rest of the UK or from differences among the population, irrespective of where they live. This decomposition provides highly valuable information to policymakers. If the inhabitants of London were to have entirely different income levels from those in the rest of the UK (and this is considered to be a problem; see Chapter 5), it would make sense to focus on regional economic, rather than nationwide, development. But, if inequality in the UK mainly follows from significant income differences between groups regardless of where they live, it would be more appropriate to direct policies toward specific subgroups generically.

Theil's T is also a popular alternative to the Gini coefficient because there is no need for individual-level income data to calculate inequality with this measure. Aggregated data, such as the average per income class, is enough. Nevertheless, Theil's T index is more difficult to interpret than the Gini coefficient, and its values cannot be compared directly across time and space. While the minimum value of Theil's T index is also 0 in case of a completely equal distribution of income across a population, its maximum value depends on the size of the population. In other words:when the population is larger, the value of Theil's T is larger, too.[5] Thus, a direct comparison of the Theil's T index for different groups leads to incorrect interpretations.[6]

Thus, the different measures of inequality shed light on the skewness of the income distribution differently and, therefore, using more than one measure contributes to obtaining a better picture of the level of income inequality in a city.

How to measure segregation

Generally speaking, income segregation is the degree to which two groups with different income levels live separately from one another in different parts of the city (Massey & Denton, 1988). Income inequality and segregation of income groups in cities are causally related: without inequality, there is no segregation (see Chapter 1). When income is not equally distributed across households in a city, differences in characteristics of neighbourhoods (e.g. house prices, proximity to amenities) ensure that some neighbourhoods are mainly populated by households with above average incomes, while households with below average incomes primarily live in other neighborhoods. Thus, segregation by income is the spatial outcome of economic inequality within a city mediated by other factors such as urban planning and the housing system (see Chapter 2).

The dissimilarity index

The most common way to measure segregation is the 'dissimilarity index' (see Appendix for the formula). In fact, the use of this measure is so common that it is often referred to as the 'segregation index' (e.g. Tammaru, Marcińczak, van Ham, & Musterd, 2016). The dissimilarity index is a measure of the 'evenness' with which two identified groups are distributed across geographical components (e.g. census tracts, postal codes, neighbourhoods) that, together, make up a larger geographical area (e.g. city, municipality, metropolitan area). Thus, in case of economic segregation, it measures how evenly low-income (or high-income) households are distributed across the neighbourhoods of a city in comparison to the same distribution of all households with an income above (or below) the low-income boundary.

To calculate the dissimilarity index, the researcher has to make two choices. First, two groups have to be identified: the minority group for which he or she wants to measure the level of segregation and the group whose distribution across the geographical units is used as a reference. In case of income differences among households, this implies dividing the population into two groups based on some chosen income boundary. The second choice is the spatial unit of measurement; that is, the geographical subunit across which the members of the minority and majority groups are distributed.

The value of the dissimilarity index can be interpreted as the proportion of the minority group that needs to be reallocated in order to obtain the same distribution of the minority group as the distribution of the reference group across the neighbourhoods of a city (UNESCO, 2017).[7] Imagine, for instance, that the value of the dissimilarity index is 0.3 for the distribution of low-income households against all households with an income above the low-income boundary. This means that 30 per cent of all low-income households living in the city should move to another neighbourhood – assuming there are no limitations, such as a limited availability of affordable houses – to make the distribution of low-income households across the city's neighbourhoods the same as that of all other households.

The value of the dissimilarity index varies between 0 and 1. In our example, a value of 0 indicates that the distribution of the low-income households and all other households are perfectly equal – there is no segregation of low-income households at the neighbourhood level. The other extreme is a situation of complete segregation (a value of 1^8), where, in one or several neighbourhoods, all households belong to the low-income group while, in all other neighbourhoods, no low-income households live at all. Thus, the higher the value of the dissimilarity index, the less similar the distribution of the two populations.

While the dissimilarity index is easy to compute and has a clear and simple interpretation, it has several shortcomings. Here, we discuss two types of shortcomings: those related to choices made within the index itself and the choice of the dissimilarity index as an indicator of segregation.

Sensitivity to measurement choices

We focus on those shortcomings that have the largest implications for a meaningful understanding of segregation in urban areas: the lack of sensitivity to the size of the minority population and limited comparability across places and time.[9] We illustrate these limitations using a simple example of the distribution of low-income households and all other households across the three neighbourhoods of a fictive city (see Figure 3.3). The picture at the top shows how 200 low-income households (minority group) and 200 households with an income above the low-income boundary (reference group) live distributed across three neighbourhoods. While both groups are the same size, their geographical distribution across the neighbourhoods differs. For this situation, the dissimilarity index has a value of 0.6, i.e., 60% of all the members of the low-income group should be redistributed to obtain a distribution across the three neighbourhoods similar to that of the neighbourhood with higher income households.

The picture on the bottom left of Figure 3.3 shows the insensitivity of the dissimilarity index to the size of the minority group. When we lower the number of low-income households in each neighbourhood (without changing their distribution across the neighbourhoods), this does not change the value of the dissimilarity index.

Generally, this lack of sensitivity to the size of the minority group is considered to be an advantage of the dissimilarity index, because it makes it possible to compare the values of groups with different sizes. However, when using the dissimilarity index in a policy context, it could also be a disadvantage. In theory, the level of segregation can be rather high, while the magnitude (i.e., number of people belonging to the minority group) is rather small.[10]

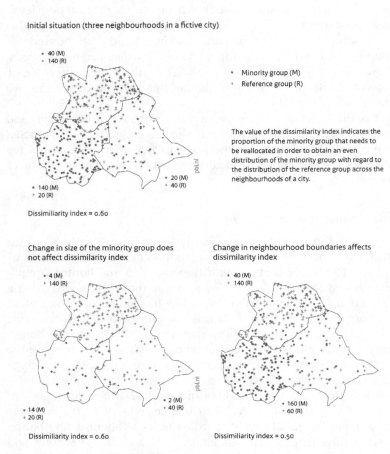

Initial situation (three neighbourhoods in a fictive city)

• 40 (M)
+ 140 (R)

• Minority group (M)
+ Reference group (R)

The value of the dissimilarity index indicates the proportion of the minority group that needs to be reallocated in order to obtain an even distribution of the minority group with regard to the distribution of the reference group across the neighbourhoods of a city.

• 20 (M)
+ 40 (R)

• 140 (M)
+ 20 (R)

Dissimiliarity index = 0.60

Change in size of the minority group does not affect dissimilarity index

• 4 (M)
+ 140 (R)

• 2 (M)
+ 40 (R)

• 14 (M)
+ 20 (R)

Dissimiliarity index = 0.60

Change in neighbourhood boundaries affects dissimilarity index

• 40 (M)
+ 140 (R)

• 160 (M)
+ 60 (R)

Dissimiliarity index = 0.50

Figure 3.3 Limitations of the dissimilarity index.

Another shortcoming of the dissimilarity index, especially when used to measure income segregation, is the limited comparability of its values across space and time. The limited comparability results from the need to choose an income boundary and a geographical subunit.

Values of the dissimilarity index can only be compared when studies apply the same income boundary to distinguish between the minority and majority groups. However, there are no rules about which boundary is most suitable. This depends on the research focus (segregation of the poor or of the rich, for instance), the research context (who is considered to be poor or rich very much differs between developed and developing countries) and the preferences of the researcher. As a corollary, the chosen income boundaries range widely between studies, hampering the comparability of research findings. This limitation led to adjustments to the original dissimilarity index (see Reardon, 2011 for an overview).

In a similar vein, differences in the choice of the geographical subunit (the neighbourhood) across which the minority and majority groups are distributed complicate comparisons of the values of the dissimilarity index. Because the dissimilarity index requires aggregating individual- or household-level income data to geographical subunits, the index is sensitive to the so-called modifiable areal unit problem (MAUP) (Openshaw & Taylor, 1981), a problem that we also illustrate in Figure 3.3.

As the picture on the bottom right illustrates, we could reach very different conclusions about the level of income segregation in this city by changing nothing else than the administrative neighbourhood boundaries. In this picture, each household still lives at the exact same location within the city, but two neighbourhoods have been merged to one subunit. Although no one moved homes, this adaptation results in a drop in the value of the dissimilarity index from 0.6 to 0.5.[11]

Hence, a meaningful comparison of the values of the dissimilarity index across cities requires using the same geographical division in both cities. Ideally, the boundaries of the spatial subareas should reflect boundaries of more or less socially coherent communities. Households living in the same neighbourhood should have more in common than two households living in other neighbourhoods, even when they live across the street from one another. However, in practice, this is very difficult to accomplish with predefined statistical areas.

Limits to the scope

The dissimilarity index measures the 'evenness' of the distribution of two groups across neighbourhoods. But, as Massey and Denton (1988) have pointed out, people can live apart or be segregated in a variety of ways. Besides evenness, other dimensions of segregation exist (exposure and clustering[12]), for which alternative statistics have been developed. Those statistics may be more suitable, depending on why one is interested in the segregation of certain groups.

An often-mentioned reason why policymakers are interested in segregation of low-income groups is the expected negative consequences of a lack of contact with other groups living in the city (see Chapter 4 for a discussion on this). When the probability of interaction between groups is the focus of interest, it is more important to measure exposure (the extent to which members of different groups share common residential areas, such as neighbuorhoods, within a city) than – as Massey and Denton (1988) put it – the abstract ideal of 'evenness' of the distribution of both groups across neighbourhoods.

The most common indicators for measuring exposure are the interaction and isolation index. While the dissimilarity index focuses on the spatial distribution of two groups, the interaction and isolation index intend to capture the social distance and possibilities of interaction between the two groups (Johnston, Poulsen, & Forrest et al., 2005). This is also why, contrary to the dissimilarity index, the latter two indices are sensitive to changes in the size of the minority group. No matter how evenly the minority group is distributed, their level of exposure to members of the majority group is likely to be higher when they form a relatively small part of the total population of the city (Blau, 1977).

Both the dissimilarity index and the interaction (or isolation) index are unable to measure the third dimension of segregation: the spatial clustering of the minority group in contiguous neighbourhoods (Wong, 2002). Measures of evenness and exposure look at to what extent members of the minority and majority groups live side by side within neighbourhoods – that is, the composition of the neighbourhood – but not how those neighbourhoods are (spatially) situated in relation to one another.

White (1983) referred to this as the 'checkerboard problem'. If the members of the minority and majority groups live completely segregated and those neighbourhoods are scattered across the city, the pattern looks like a checkerboard (the picture on the left in Figure 3.4). If members of both groups were to move to other neighbourhoods to live closer to members of their own group, the pattern would change to the picture on the right: neighbourhoods where the minority group lives surrounded by other neighbourhoods with a high concentration of minority members. However, such a shift has no effect on the value of the dissimilarity or the interaction index.

The level of spatial clustering attracts a lot of attention from policymakers because they consider contiguous concentration areas of minority groups to be more problematic as these could intensify the problems associated with a lack of evenness or interaction between groups (see Chapter 4, section 'The negative impact of economic segregation'). That is why much effort is put into developing so-called spatial autocorrelation techniques that measure concentration of groups in·neighbourhoods while taking into account their level of concentration in bordering neighbourhoods (Anselin, 1995).

More recently, even more advanced techniques were introduced that enable measuring segregation on the individual or household level (e.g. Oka & Wong, 2016). With information on the exact locations of

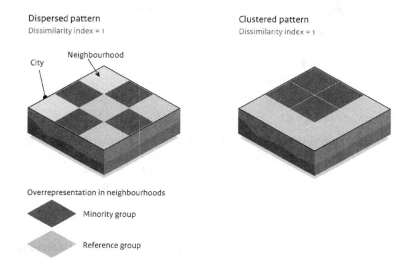

Figure 3.4 Dispersed and clustered segregation.
Source: Wong, D. W. S. (1993).

individuals (their residential addresses), individualised neighbourhoods can be defined that measure how close each individual lives to those belonging to the same or other groups (Östh, Malmberg & Andersson, 2014). This method also improves the comparability of segregation values across cities and countries, because it helps to overcome the difficulties related to the modifiable area unit problem.

In this chapter, we focused on *residential* segregation, while other forms of segregation beyond the residential environment are relevant and have been explored in recent studies as well. Individuals' social interactions are not limited to where people live but also take place in other places where they conduct daily activities such as working, recreating, etc. (Krivo et al., 2013; Li & Wang, 2017).

Inequality and segregation of what?

Until now, we wrote about measuring inequality and segregation by income without making explicit what we meant by income. However, income is not as straightforward as it may seem. Simply put, the income of an individual or household is the sum of all earnings someone received within a certain period of time. Because those earnings can come from different sources, a whole range of income definitions exist.

The definition used affects both the levels of income inequality or segregation measured and the part of the population that is included (OECD, 2011). Furthermore, economic inequality can be measured by other indicators than income. Since the publication of Piketty's *Capital*, differences in capital have received increasing attention. This raises the question of inequality and segregation of *what*?

Wage, income or capital

Economic inequality can be expressed by wage, income or capital (see List of Concepts for definitions). But, it is important to note that wage, income and capital of individuals are three different things that may overlap to some extent and for certain groups of individuals.

Wage or income

Income is broader than wage. While wage is how much an individual earns through working as an employee, income consists of wage(s) *plus* the profits of having your own company, social benefits and rents from capital (savings, stock exchange investments, etc.). For several reasons, inequality is generally larger when measured by income than by wage. First, additional income sources create more variety on top of differences in wages among the same group of individuals.

Second, studies on wage inequality are often interested in differences in 'pay for work'. To correct for differences in the number of hours worked, these studies only compare hourly wages of full-time workers or recalculate wages to the equivalent of full-time workers (the wage someone would have earned if working full-time). In studies on income inequality, such adjustments are not made, which leads to more variance in incomes between part-time and full-time workers. As a consequence, income inequality is generally larger than wage inequality. In Amsterdam, for instance, the Gini coefficient measured for personal incomes was 0.32 in 2012, but, when measured in hourly wages, was only 0.28 for an identical group of workers.

Third, the number of individuals in a city who receive an income is larger than those who receive an income primarily from employment. Employees are the only individuals who receive a wage. Individuals who earn an income can be employees, but can also be self-employed, unemployed or disabled people receiving social benefits, or non-workers earning a pension, interest payments or rents. These differences imply that measuring (changes in) inequality and segregation for different

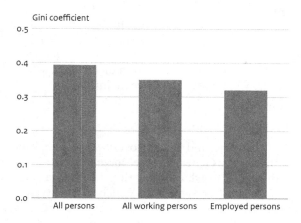

Gini coefficient

Figure 3.5 Income inequality among three groups living in Amsterdam, 2012.

income definitions can lead to different conclusions. Even more because income differences tend to be larger among those who do not receive income from employment, as Figure 3.5 illustrates for the city of Amsterdam. When we include all persons with an income, the value of the Gini coefficient is clearly higher than when we measure income inequality among all working persons (employed plus self-employed) or only among employed persons.

Income or capital

An individual's capital or wealth is the balance between that person's financial and material possessions and his or her debts. Although we consider income and capital as analytically distinct, they are closely related in practice (van Bavel & Frankema, 2013). High income earners have more opportunities to save part of their income and, thus, to accumulate more capital. Reversely, more capital generates additional income through higher interest and rents from capital.

The distribution of capital is generally more skewed than that of income. There are several reasons for this (van Bavel & Frankema, 2013). First, capital is a stock that allows for indefinite accumulation, while income earnings are flows that are naturally limited. Furthermore, incomes are rarely negative (except for the self-employed), while it is quite common to have a net debt position. As a result, the range of a capital distribution tends to be wider than that of income.

From gross incomes to standard of living

Researchers interested in economic inequality and segregation often look for a measure that reflects differences in the standard of living across households. While income is often used as an indicator, different choices can be made both in the definition of income itself and in alternatives to income. We describe the three main choices.

Market or disposable incomes

Through social transfers and taxes, governments redistribute income among their inhabitants. Generally, three income types are distinguished that differ with regard to what extent they take these social transfers and taxes into account (see Table 3.1). Which income type is most suitable depends on the research question: primary incomes provide better insights into inequality within the labour market, while disposable incomes are a good indicator of differences in consumption options.

Because lower-income groups usually pay less tax and receive more social benefits, inequality is considerably smaller when measured by disposable incomes instead of market incomes. In countries with an extensive redistribution policy, the difference can be substantial. In Germany in 2010, for instance, the Gini coefficient had a value of 0.41 when measured for market incomes and only 0.28 for disposable incomes across the working-age population, compared to values of 0.36 and 0.33 for both income types in Italy (Gornick, Milanovic, & Johnson, 2017). Therefore, it is important for studies on income inequality (and segregation of

Table 3.1 Different types of income and inequality

Income type	Components	Income inequality
Primary or market income	Gross wages and salaries + self-employment income + cash property income + occupational and private pensions + private transfers + other cash income	Income inequality before social transfers and taxes
Gross income	+ Social security cash benefits	Income inequality before taxes
Secondary or disposable income	-/- Payroll (mandatory payroll taxes) -/- income taxes	Income inequality after social transfers and taxes

Source: Wang C., and Caminada C. L. J. 2011.

income groups) to make clear which taxes and social transfers are taken into account and which are not.

Individual or household level

While differences in wages or market incomes are commonly measured at the individual level, it makes more sense to measure disposable income inequality at the household level. Members of the same household generally pool their income and, in this way, benefit from the economies of scale of running a household together (by sharing costs for housing, food, childcare, etc.) (Salverda et al., 2013). Furthermore, certain social transfers and taxes are paid by household and not individually (for instance, cost of housing, childcare), or the benefits depend on the household composition. For instance, in the Netherlands, the amount of social benefits for the long-term unemployed depends on the income of the people with whom they share a household.

However, households differ in size and in the number of people earning an income. Such differences affect the level of income inequality and, as explained in Chapter 2, may also explain an increase in income inequality. As these differences can hardly be influenced by policy, researchers may want to measure the level of inequality without these differences influencing the picture. One option is to limit the analysis to those who belong to the same household type or to standardise household incomes by making the income of all households comparable to that of one type; for instance, single-person households (Salverda, 2013).

Standard of living = income – daily cost of living

Although many studies use income as an indicator of differences in the standard of living across households, incomes do not provide an accurate picture of the geographical differences in standard of living because they do not take into account differences in cost of living (Moretti, 2013). For instance, in the economic 'powerhouses' of the last decades, such as New York and London, incomes have risen extremely fast, but this growth was accompanied by booming house prices and higher prices of consumption goods (Glaeser, Gyourko, & Saks, 2005). As a consequence, the real income of the inhabitants of those cities is substantially smaller than their nominal income.[13] Using differences in housing costs as an indicator of geographical differences in the cost of living, Moretti (2010) showed that, in cities such as San Jose, Stanford and San Francisco, the real income is more than 20% below the nominal income when those cities' extremely high costs of living in are taken into account. In cities such as Gadsen, Anniston and Johnstown, on the other hand, real income is more than 15% above the nominal income. However, the latter places offer fewer amenities than the former. Having access to amenities can also be said to contribute to one's standard of living.

Incomes corrected for differences in cost of living only provide insights into *material* living standards. General well-being, quality of life or happiness is affected by more than the number of goods someone can buy (see also Chapter 5). In fact, people may consciously choose a less demanding job or work fewer hours to have more time to spend on other activities that they consider to be important. While this may lower their income and resources for consumption, it may in fact contribute to their quality of life. In 2013, 38 per cent of all employees in the Netherlands worked fewer than 30 hours a week[14], followed by Switzerland, Australia and the UK at about 25 per cent of all employees (OECD, 2017).

A dynamic perspective on inequality and segregation

Studies on dynamics in inequality and segregation often compare yearly snapshots of the income distribution in a city. Each year, the Gini coefficient or dissimilarity index is measured using information on the incomes and residential locations of everyone who lives in the city at that time, a procedure that is repeated for a series of years. However, inequality goes beyond the variations seen in year-on-year income (Stiglitz, 2012, p. 3). Although such yearly numbers shed light on the overall development of inequality and segregation, they remain (static) snapshots that miss essential information about the underlying dynamics.

Yearly snapshots of income inequality do not tell us anything about who belongs to the poor and rich in which year. The 'poor' of the first year may not be the same persons as the 'poor' in later years. In a similar way, new groups may reach the top of the income distribution over time, while others lose their top positons. Incomes evolve during the course of people's lives and, as a result, individuals or households can ascend (or descend) the income ladder. If who belongs to which income group is not fixed over time, inequality is much different from a situation in which the same persons are the poor year after year.

Measures of income inequality cannot grasp the long-term evolution of households along the income ladder; that is, the level of income *mobility*. In essence, yearly snapshots of the Gini coefficient or other income inequality statistics are cross-sectional in nature, as each year a different sample of households is compared. Measuring income mobility asks for a longitudinal approach in which the income position of the same set of individuals is tracked over time (Jäntti & Jenkins, 2015).

Figure 3.6 demonstrates the difference between income inequality and income mobility and the added value of the latter. This figure shows both the income distribution in 2003 of the main household earners who lived in Amsterdam and were 30–35 years old in that year, and the income distribution in 2012 for exactly the same group. Through connecting the position of each individual in 2003 with that in 2012, their income mobility becomes clear. To correct for structural changes in the income distribution of the Netherlands (e.g. a general rise in the average income), we do not compare actual income levels but the position of the selected group of individuals in the 10 deciles of the income distribution.[15] Thus, we look at changes in the *relative* income position of each individual. All individuals with an income below the income level of the 10th percentile belong to the lowest income group (decile 1), and those with an income above the 90th percentile to the highest (decile 10).

When we measure the Gini coefficient for the income distributions of 2003 and 2012, the value for 2012 is higher than the one for 2003 (see Figure 3.6). Thus, income inequality among this group has increased. However, if we look at individuals' positions within the income distribution, we see that 54 per cent have ascended to a higher income decile, 26 per cent have descended to a lower income decile and 20 per cent have stayed in the same decile.[16] Thus, there is quite some mobility among

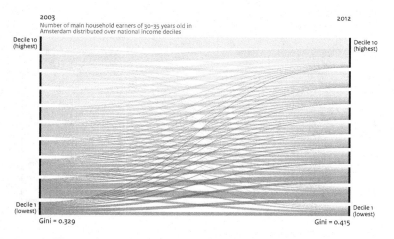

Figure 3.6 Changes in relative income position, 2003–2012.
Source: Statistics Netherlands 2017 (edited by the authors).

people who lived in Amsterdam in 2003, and the majority of it is up the social ladder. Downward movements are also not limited to the lower income groups: 22 per cent of those who belonged to the highest-income decile in 2003 had a lower income position in 2012.

The same reasoning applies to segregation: yearly snapshots of the dissimilarity index provide no information about which neighbourhood has the highest concentration of poor (or rich) and obscure residential mobility. Changes in income position, but also in household situation, trigger individuals to move between neighbourhoods. Selective in- and out migration leads to a constantly changing population composition of neighbourhoods (van Ham, Manley, Bailey, Simpson, & Maclennan, 2013). As a consequence, which neighbourhoods have the largest concentrations of poor (or rich) may change over time.

And, even when one neighbourhood always contains the largest concentration of people in the lowest income decile, we have a different situation when this group renews and changes every year from when it remains (virtually) the same group. By focusing on the residential mobility of individuals, it becomes clear to what extent the inhabitants of the poorest neighbourhood have the opportunity to leave that neighbourhood and move to better parts of the city and, thus, climb up the residential ladder. Yearly segregation snapshots provide no insights into these neighbourhood dynamics.

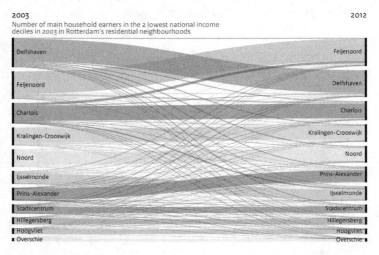

Figure 3.7 Changes in residential location of low-income inhabitants of Rotterdam, 2003–2012.

Source: Statistics Netherlands 2017 (edited by the authors).

Similar to income mobility, insight into residential mobility asks for a longitudinal approach in which the same group of people is followed over time. Figure 3.7 illustrates the type of insights such an approach can provide. This example visualises the neighbourhood careers of main household earners who, in 2003, had a low income (20 per cent lowest incomes nationally) across 11 neighbourhoods in the second largest city of the Netherlands, Rotterdam. Clearly, the residential mobility of this group is very limited: 77 per cent lived in the same neighbourhood in 2012 as in 2003. Furthermore, while 13 per cent did move to a neighbourhood with a lower share of low-income households, almost 10 per cent moved to a neighbourhood with a higher share of low-income inhabitants.

Figures 3.6 and 3.7 are both illustrations of intragenerational mobility: the same people are followed over time. Other studies emphasised the importance of looking at intergenerational mobility, that is, the extent to which parental income positions predetermine the opportunities and the income position of their children (e.g. Solon 1992; Björklund & Jäntti 2009; Jäntti & Jenkins, 2015). Both types of mobility studies look at the interdependence between origins and destinations of individuals. However, if that relation is the main focus of the research, it may make more sense to look at intergenerational mobility, because the parental background is something over which individuals had no choice while they can affect their future development through life choices they make early on, such as the decision to follow an education (Jäntti and Jenkins 2015). These studies are part of investigating 'equality of opportunity' instead of 'equality of outcomes' (see Chapter 5).

In the case of spatial segregation, it is also worthwhile to study the interdependence in neighbourhood careers of parents and children to see whether some neighbourhoods really function as 'spatial poverty traps' (e.g. Grant, 2010; van Ham, Hedman, Manley, Coulters, & Östh, 2014). Following neighbourhoods over time, and following (generations of) people in neighbourhoods over time, provides us with more information about whether 'slums' are 'perpetual' or are prone to processes of 'unslumming' (Jacobs, 1961) and to what extent people have the opportunity to move up the residential ladder.

Appendix

Measuring inequality and segregation

$$\text{Gini coefficient} = 1 - \sum_{i=1} (x_i - x_{i-1})(y_i + y_{i-1})$$

Where:
N: size of the population,
x: share of total population (x-axis of the Lorenz curve), and
y: share of total income (y-axis of the Lorenz curve).

$$\text{Dissimilarity index} = \frac{1}{2} \sum_{i=1}^{N} \left| \frac{l_i}{L} - \frac{o_i}{O} \right|.$$

where (in case of comparing a low-income group with all other inhabitants of a city):
l_i = the low-income population of the ith area (e.g. a neighbourhood),
L = the total low-income population of the large geographic entity (city) for which the index of dissimilarity is being calculated,
o_i = the population with an income above the low-income boundary of the ith area, and
O = the population with an income above the low-income boundary of the large geographic entity for which the index of dissimilarity is being calculated.

Notes

1 Multiplying the measure with the same constant does not affect the level of inequality.

2 It should be kept in mind, however, that comparing Gini coefficients across cities (or regions and countries) is not without limitations. Larger countries are often economically more diverse than smaller countries. Consequently, the Gini coefficient still tends to be higher for larger countries such as the United States than for smaller European countries.

3 As large differences in income may exist among the people that belong to the same decile or percentile, ratio statistics often compare the mean incomes instead of bound values (e.g., the mean income of the 10 per cent poorest and richest persons, the S90:S10 ratio).

4 Theil's T is the most often-used measure of the family of generalised entropy inequality measures that can all be decomposed into subgroups (World Bank 2005). Entropy measures were developed in information theory as a measure of redundancy in data. Theil's T index indicates the maximum possible entropy of the data minus the observed entropy. In information theory, this index is interpreted as non-randomness, which, in studies of income distribution, is translated to inequality (but also segregation). Generalised entropy measures include a sensitivity parameter that can take different values, enabling researchers to measure inequality while being more sensitive to differences at the top (parameter of 1 and 2) or at the bottom of the distribution (parameter of -1). Theil's T index has a sensitivity parameter of 1. Another often-used generalised entropy measure is Theil's L, or the mean log deviation measure (sensitivity parameter of 0).

5 The same goes for the number of groups that are distinguished (in case of aggregated income data). It is not possible to directly compare the Theil's T index measured for the 50 states of the United States with that for the 10 provinces of Canada. According to Theil (1967), this is an important characteristic of this measure as a group of people consisting of two persons with only one of them earning all the income is intuitively less unequal than the same distribution among a larger group of people.

6 It is, however, possible to compare the Theil's T index for two populations with different sizes by dividing the value of each population first by its maximum value. This generates a relative entropy inequality index that varies between 0 and 1 and for which a value of 0.2 indicates that the inequality is 20 per cent of the maximum inequality as measured by the Theil index.

7 Similar to the Gini coefficient, the dissimilarity index can be derived from the Lorenz curve (see Figure 3.1). In the case of segregation, the cumulative proportion of the minority group is plotted against the cumulative proportion of the majority group across the neighbourhoods of the city. The dissimilarity index represents the maximum distance of the Lorenz curve to the diagonal line of perfect evenness.

8 If all low income households are concentrated in neighbourhoods with no members of the reference group, all low income households have to move to another neighbourhood to achieve an even share of low income households in all neighbourhoods.

9 Other shortcomings are that the dissimilarity index does not fulfill the 'transfer principle,' which states that a measure should be sensitive to the

redistribution of minorities among areal units with minority proportions above or below the metropolitan area's minority proportion. To overcome this limitation, several authors prefer to use the Gini coefficient instead. Another shortcoming is the inability to measure segregation of multiple groups, which is why some argue it is better to use the Theil index.

10 To deal with this issue, Ponds et al. (2015) developed the so-called 'moving index' which indicates to what extent a large share of inhabitants of the city lives segregated or not. This index takes the perspective of the city as a whole and, hence, may have a very low value even when all members of the minority group live in one neighbourhood, but the group forms only a small share of the total number of inhabitants.

11 For comparable examples in non-fictive cities, see Wong, Laus & Falk (1999).

12 Massey and Denton (1988) made a distinction in five subgroups: evenness, exposure, concentration, centralization and clustering. However, later conceptual studies on segregation consider concentration and centralization as two subcategories of clustering in which the degree of clustering is measured relative to a specific part of the urban area (e.g., city centre).

13 Although, on the other hand, options for capital accumulation are also greater in those places.

14 Note that working part time is not always a voluntary choice, but may also be an indication of a precarious job, as we explain in Chapter 2.

15 All individuals who were head of their household in the Netherlands were sorted by their income level and divided into 10 groups of equal size for the years 2003 and 2012 separately.

16 Remember that this may not imply a lower income, as what we compare is their relative position on the income distribution, and incomes in general may have increased.

References

Allison, P. D. (1978). Measures of inequality. *American Sociological Review*, *43*(6), 865–880.

Anselin, L. (1995). Local indicators of spatial association – LISA. *Geographical Analysis*, *27*(2), 93–115.

Atkinson, A. B. (1975). *The Economics of Inequality*. Oxford, UK: Oxford University Press.

Björklund, A., & Jäntti, M. (2009). Intergenerational income mobility and the role of family background. In W. Salverda, B. Nolan, & T. M. Smeeding (Eds.), *Oxford Handbook of Economic Inequality* (pp. 491–521). Oxford, UK: Oxford University Press.

Blau, P. M. (1977). *Inequality and Heterogeneity: A Primitive Theory of Social Structure*. New York, NY: Free Press.

de Maio, F. G. (2007). Income inequality measures. *Journal of Epidemiology & Community Health*, *61*(10), 849–852.

Dorling, D. (2014). *Inequality and the 1%*. London, UK: Verso.

Glaeser, E. L., Gyourko, J., & Saks, R. (2005). Why is Manhattan so expensive? Regulation and the rise in house prices. *Journal of Law and Economics*, *48*(2), 331–370.

Grant, U. (2010). Spatial inequality and urban poverty traps. ODI/CPRC Working Paper Series No. WP326 (ODI), No. WP166 (CPRC). Overseas Development Institute, https://www.odi.org/sites/odi.org.uk/files/odi-assets/publications-opinion-files/5502.pdf

Gornick, J. C., Milanovic, B., & Johnson, N. (2017). American exceptionalism in market income inequality: An analysis based on microdata from the Luxembourg Income Study (LIS) database. LIS Working Paper No. 692. LIS: Cross-National Data Center in Luxembourg, www.lisdatacenter.org/wps/liswps/692.pdf

Jacobs, J. (1961). *The Death and Life of Great American Cities*. New York, NY: Random House.

Jäntti, M., & Jenkins, S. P. (2015). Income mobility. In A. Atkinson & T. Bourguignon (Eds.), *Handbook of Income Distribution* (Vol. 2A, pp. 807–935). Amsterdam, the Netherlands: Springer.

Johnston, R., Poulsen, M., & Forrest, J. (2005). On the measurement and meaning of residential segregation: A response to Simpson. *Urban Studies*, *42*(7), 1221–1227.

Krivo, L. J., Washington, H. M., Peterson, R. D., Browning, C. R., Calder, C. A., & Kwan, M. P. (2013). Social isolation of disadvantage and advantage: The reproduction of inequality in urban space. *Social forces*, *92*(1), 141–164.

Li, F. and Wang, D. (2017). Measuring urban segregation based on daily activity patterns: A multidimensional approach. *Environment and Planning A*, *49*(2), 467–486.

Massey, D. S., & Denton, N. A. (1988). The dimensions of residential segregation. *Social Forces*, *67*(2), 281–315.

Moretti, E. (2010). Poverty, inequality and cost of living differences. Research Discussion Paper Series No. DP2010-07. University of Kentucky Center for Poverty Research, www.ukcpr.org/Publications/DP2010-07.pdf

Moretti, E. (2013). Real wage inequality. *American Economic Journal: Applied Economics*, *5*(1), 65–103.

OECD. (2011). Divided we stand: Why inequality keeps rising. Paris, France: OECD.

OECD. (2017, March 10). Labour market statistics 2013: Full-time part-time employment - common definition: Incidence. https://data.oecd.org/emp/part-time-employment-rate.htm

Oka, M., & Wong, D. W. S. (2016). Spatializing area-based measures of neighbourhood characteristics for multilevel regression analyses: An areal median filtering approach. *Journal of Urban Health*, *93*(3), 551–571.

Openshaw, S., & Taylor, P. J. (1981). The modifiable areal unit problem. In N. Wrigley and R. J. Bennett (Eds.), *Quantitative Geography: A British View* (pp. 60–69). London, UK: Routledge and Kegan Paul.

Östh, J., Malmberg, B., & Andersson, E. K. (2014). Analysing segregation using individualised neighbourhoods. In L. D. Christopher, I. G. Shuttleworth, & D. W. Wong (Ed.), *Socio-Spatial Segregation: Concepts, Processes and Outcomes* (pp. 135–162). Bristol, UK: Policy Press.

Piketty, T. (2014). *Capital in the Twenty-First Century*. Cambridge, MA: University Press.

Ponds, R., Marlet, G., van Woerkens, C., & van Ham, M. (2015). *Measures of segregation: background and differences*. Utrecht, the Netherlands: Atlas voor Gemeenten.

Reardon, S. F. (2011). Measures of income segregation. CEPA Working Paper. Stanford Center on Poverty and Inequality, http://inequality.stanford.edu/sites/default/files/reardon_measures-income-seg.pdf

Salverda, W. (2011). The Netherlands: Is the impact of the financial crisis on inequalities different from in the past? In D. Vaughan-Whitehead (Ed.), *Inequalities in the World of Work: The Effects of the Crisis* (pp. 355–396). Geneva, Switzerland: Edward Elgar and International Labour Organisation.

Salverda, W. (2013). Income, redistribution and household formation 1977–2011: 35 years of growth in income inequality in the Netherlands. *TPEdigitaal*, 7(1), 66–94.

Salverda, W., & Atkinson, A. B. (2007). Top incomes in the Netherlands over the twentieth century. In A. B. Atkinson and T. Piketty (Eds.), *Top Incomes over the Twentieth Century: A Contrast between Continental European and English-Speaking Countries* (pp. 426–471). Oxford, UK: Oxford University Press.

Salverda, W., Haas, C., de Graaf-Zijl, M., Lancee, B., Notten, N., & Ooms, T. (2013). *Growing Inequalities and Their Impacts in the Netherlands*. GINI Country Reports. Amsterdam, the Netherlands: GINI.

Shorrocks, A. F. (1980). The class of additively decomposable inequality measures. *Econometrica*, 48(3), 613–625.

Solon, G. (1992). Intergenerational income mobility in the United States. *American Economic Review*, 82(3), 393–408.

Stiglitz, J. E. (2012). The price of inequality: How today's divided society endangers our future. New York, NY: W. W. Norton & Company.

Tammaru, T., Marcińczak, S., van Ham, M., & Musterd, S. (Eds.). (2016). *Socio-Economic Segregation in European Capital Cities*. London, UK: Routledge.

Theil, H. (1967). *Economics and Information Theory*. Chicago, IL: Rand McNally.

UNESCO. (2017). Dissimilarity index. http://uis.unesco.org/en/glossary-term/dissimilarity-index

van Bavel, B., & Frankema, E. (2013). Low income inequality, high wealth inequality. The puzzle of the Rhineland welfare states. CGEH Working Paper Series No. 50. Centre for Global Economic History, www.cgeh.nl/sites/default/files/WorkingPapers/CGEHWP50_vanbavelfrankema.pdf

van Ham, M., Manley, D., Bailey, N., Simpson, L., & Maclennan, D. (2013). Understanding neighbourhood dynamics: New insights for neighbourhood effects research. In M. van Ham, D. Manley, N. Bailey, L. Simpson, & D. MacLennan (Eds.), *Understanding Neighbourhood Dynamics: New Insights for Neighbourhood Effects Research* (pp. 1–21). Dordrecht, the Netherlands: Springer.

van Ham, M., Hedman, L., Manley, D., Coulter, R., & Östh, J. (2014). Intergenerational transmission of neighbourhood poverty: An analysis of neighbourhood histories of individuals. *Transactions of the Institute of British Geographers, 39*(3), 402–417.

Wang, C., & Caminada, C. L. J. (2011). Disentangling income inequality and the redistributive effect of social transfers and taxes in 36 LIS countries. Department of Economics Research Memorandum No. 2011.02. Leiden Law School, http://media.leidenuniv.nl/legacy/rm-2011-02.pdf

White, M. J. (1983). The measurement of spatial segregation. *American Journal of Sociology, 88*(5), 1008–1018.

Wong, D. W. S. (1993). Spatial indices of segregation. *Urban Studies, 30*(3), 559–572.

Wong, D. W. S. (2002). Modelling local segregation: A spatial interaction approach. *Geographical and Environmental Modelling, 6*(1), 81–97.

Wong, D. W. S., Laus, H., & Falk, R. F. (1999). Exploring the variability of segregation index D with scale and zonal systems: An analysis of thirty US cities. *Environment and Planning A, 31*(3), 507–522.

World Bank. (2005). Inequality measures. In World Bank (Ed.), *Handbook on Poverty and Inequality* (pp. 105–120). Washington, DC: World Bank.

World Bank. (2016). *Poverty and Shared Prosperity 2016: Taking on Inequality.* Washington, DC: World Bank.

4 Reflecting on the (negative) societal impact

> A house may be large or small; as long as the neighbouring houses are likewise small, it satisfies all social requirement for a residence. But let there arise next to the little house a palace, and the little house shrinks to a hut.
> —Karl Marx, Wage labour and capital, 1847

Many consider economic inequality and segregation problematic as they are claimed to produce negative social effects of various kinds. In this chapter, we explore what those may be. We will start by discussing the effects of economic inequality in the section 'The negative impact of economic inequality', and will then move on to the effects of segregation, which will be discussed in the section 'The negative impact of economic segregation'. At the outset, it is important to stress that, when looking at economic inequality, we talk about relative poverty and the skewedness of the distribution of income and wealth (again, see Chapter 3). In other words, we discuss the size of economic *differences* and the effect of *those differences* on other social phenomena. There are logical and empirical-methodological challenges to proving such an effect. However, proof is important, as we will see. In some cases, it may make more sense to link some social or economic effects to the (absolute) poverty or (absolute) richness of specific groups that together make up the economic distribution rather than to the *difference* between them (i.e. relative poverty or economic inequality).

The negative impact of economic inequality

The most prominent social phenomena that have been explored in relation to economic inequality are economic growth, health and social well-being and social cohesion. We focus on some of the more influential contributions and some important overviews on the effects of economic inequality. The literature is not necessarily 'urban' – much of it is more general. However, there is no reason to believe that most of the premises and findings do not hold at the city or regional level.

Effects on economic growth

Those who consider economic inequality to be objectionable and something that needs to be reduced often refer to the negative effects it may have on economic growth. In the literature, however, both positive and negative effects are being identified. Let us start by describing roughly four different lines of arguments, or approaches, through which it may be argued that economic inequality is detrimental to economic growth (Perotti, 1996; de Dominicis, Florax, & de Groot, 2008, pp. 656–657).

1 First, there is the argument of imperfect credit markets that disturb the economic principle of 'decreasing returns to capital'[1] (e.g. Stiglitz, 2012). It works as follows. Let us first assume that there are no borrowing constraints; credits markets function perfectly. Second, in line with the principle of decreasing return to capital, we assume that those with much capital have less return on it than those with little capital. Under the condition that everyone can borrow freely, this mechanism should, ultimately, lead to the convergence of wealth to a common level – since the poor accumulate wealth more rapidly than the rich – and should not affect aggregate output. However, in practice, credit markets are imperfect and borrowing constraints are present: it may be more difficult for poorer people to obtain credit. When those constraints are introduced, the principle of increasing returns does not work as it would in a perfect market situation. This implies that wealth convergence does not take place and that initial endowments and the initial wealth distribution play a much more significant role and result in lower productivity and a lower rate of growth (e.g. Aghion, Caroli, & García-Peñalosa, 1999, pp. 1621–1622).

2 The second argument concerns sociopolitical instability. An unequal society would lead to antisocial behaviour, such as crime, violent protests and maybe even revolutions, which may lead to insecurity and distrust. Such destabilisation discourages investment and slows down economic growth (Perotti, 1996; Stiglitz, 2012). Thus, it is the mental reaction of people and groups to income inequality that would cause less growth. The relation between economic inequality and socio-political instability is, therefore, a psychological

and not a logical one. In other words, emotional rather than along the 'formal' lines of reason (e.g. if A happens, B will happen). The extent to which this is the case in practice is an empirical question, as its presence and impact is not known in advance.

3   The third argument that is used is derived from a theoretical model in which the interdependency of the fertility rate and educational spending and its impact on economic growth is conceptualised. It is assumed that poor people tend to have more children and can therefore spend less (per child) on education. In addition, there is the assumption that more human capital enhances economic growth. It follows that, if the fertility differential between the rich and the poor is significant, more weight is put on children with little education, which reduces average educational level and, consequently, economic growth. The more wealth is concentrated in the hands of only a few people, the greater the number of people with less money, the greater the number of poorly educated children, the lower the average level of human capital and the lower the economic growth (de la Croix & Doepke, 2003).

4   The last causal reasoning focuses on the effect of fiscal policies (de Dominicis et al., 2008). The argument is that, when there is greater concentration of wealth and income in a society, the government will be inclined to take redistributive measures (e.g. expenditures and taxes) that are economically distortive and growth-diminishing. This argument is distinct as it already includes the government (fiscal) response to economic inequality. It is, therefore, not a valid (or a less valid) argument to support yet another government response, since it is the cause of the negative effect in the first place. Thus, the issue of fiscal government policies is *endogenous* rather than *exogenous*.

Alternatively, there are also scholars who argue that economic growth *benefits* from some form of economic inequality. Three categories of arguments of why economic inequality would bring forward economic growth can be distinguished (Aghion et al., 1999; de Dominicis et al. 2008, p. 656).

1   The first argument is best known and arguably the strongest of the three. It relates to incentives for work (Aghion et al., 1999, p. 1615). If people who are unequal in their ability and willingness to work are to keep the rewards they receive from making the effort, they may be encouraged to make such an effort. De Vos asks, 'What would we do if we knew that, no matter what we did, the result would always

be an even distribution of resources through redistribution?' He, himself, answers it by stating that, '...if people cannot keep their earnings, they will work less and study less; if businesses cannot celebrate success, they will not aim to be successful; if people cannot keep capital, they will save less and build less investment capital' (de Vos, 2015, p. 282 - translation authors).

2   The second argument follows from differences in saving propensity between different wealth and income groups. The marginal propensity of the rich to save is more than that of the poor, because the rich have more excess money above what they have to spend on primary needs. Assuming that the investment rate and savings rate are positively correlated, it follows that more unequal wealth and income distributions lead to more investments that foster economic growth.

3   Finally, some argue that large indivisible investments (for instance, in infrastructure) are necessary to trigger new activities and development, and require a concentration of wealth among few people. Therefore, a skewed wealth distribution toward the richer part would produce more growth.

Ambiguous causality

The above shows that, next to those who argue that economic inequality reduces economic growth, there are those who say that the latter is fostered by the former. This ambiguity is reflected in the more empirical literature. De Dominicis et al. (2008) have carried out a meta-analysis of 37 empirical studies containing 407 estimated effects of income inequality – the common proxy for economic inequality – on economic growth. They found contradictory results. On the one hand, there are many studies that do find a solid detrimental effect of income inequality on economic growth. But, more recently, with samples containing more countries and longer time spans, and with more sophisticated econometric techniques, more evidence is provided for a positive correlation. Because of that, the authors conclude that 'no general consensus has emerged so far' (p. 655).

Next to the notion that the causal effect of economic inequality on growth could be positive as well as negative, there may be two additional reasons for the lack of convincing empirical proof for either one of the two hypotheses. The first concerns changing causality over time, and the second the importance of wealth and income *levels* of people and groups rather than *differences*.

When it comes to changing causality over time, there are theories, starting as early as Simon Kuznets's hypothesis in 1955, which state that the relationship between inequality and economic growth is not stable over time and depends on the stage of development. Kuznets found that, in early stages of development, from agricultural to industrial societies, income inequality is typically low, while it rises after economic growth takes off. It decreases again once the growth slows down and the economy matures. The hypothesis has been criticised later, for instance, for its inapplicability to developed industrialised countries that, contrary to the theory, experienced rising inequalities. However, the notion of different relations between economic growth and income inequality over time has not disappeared (Aghion et al., 1999, p. 1615; de Dominicis et al., 2008, p. 656).

Some of the arguments behind either the negative effects (arguments 1 and 3) or the positive effects (arguments 2 and 3) of economic inequality are somewhat problematic from a logical point of view. Take, for instance, the third argument for the negative effects of inequality, in which it is deduced that greater economic inequality leads to a lower average education level (because of high fertility and less spending on education among the poor) and, hence, to lower growth. However, it is not the fact that others have more but the fact that poor people are poor that leads to high fertility rates and little investment in human capital among this group. They would not have fewer children or spend more on education if all others in society had the same wealth and income level as they had. The same holds for the second argument used to support *positive* growth effects of inequality. The richer people are, the greater the propensity to save and to invest savings. However, it is the rich person's own wealth and income *level* that triggers them to save, not the fact that others have less. In other words, we raise questions about whether it is the '(un)evenness' of the distribution that produces the positive or adverse effects on economic growth, and contend, instead, that economic growth is affected because some people or groups have much or little (in absolute terms).

In short, the logical reasoning behind many of the negative and the positive effects of economic inequality on economic growth is often ambiguous. The presence of social-psychological effects of economic inequality, which again can be both negative and positive, seems more plausible. Arguably, as a result of either ambiguous or contradictory causal relations, the empirical support for both the positive and the negative growth effects of economic inequality is not convincing.

Health and social effects

There are those who argue that economic inequality has negative social and health effects. The most influential book in this area so far has been *The Spirit Level* by epidemiologists Richard Wilkinson and Kate Pickett (2009). Because of their impact and readership, we discuss their argument together with some of their critics and some literature reviews, in order to reflect on the presence of a relationship between economic (i.e. income) inequality and health and social well-being.

Wilkinson and Pickett (2009) provide many statistically significant correlations between income inequality in countries on the one hand, and, on the other, health and social issues such as obesity, mental health, drug use, life expectancy, teenage births, violence, imprisonment, educational performance and social mobility. They do this for 23 developed countries and use data from the 50 US states as an additional test. The correlations that they show between income inequality and each of these factors are generally positive, strong and significant, as is the association between income inequality and an overall index of health and social problems (Figure 4.1).

They do not just claim that income inequality leads to health inequality and inequality of well-being – which most of us will readily accept as true or plausible (see also Rowlingson, 2011, pp. 8–9) – but they also argue that, with an increase in income inequality in a society, there is a decrease of overall health and well-being levels. It is not only the health and well-being of lower income groups that are adversely affected, but also those of the richer in society. The causal reasoning behind this is

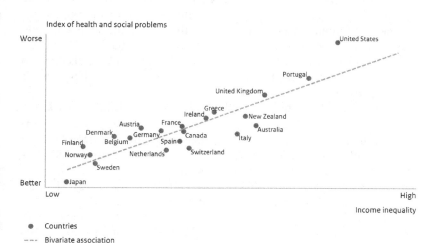

Figure 4.1 A bivariate association in 'The spirit level'.
Source: Wilkinson, R., & Pickett, K., 2009.

that, particularly in developed countries, where people worry less about staying alive than in developing countries, the evaluation of one's position in the social hierarchy has become more important. In that light, significant or growing income inequality leads to status anxiety and insecurity for both the poor *and* the rich. In effect, as Wilkinson and Pickett (2009) argue, this, on average, leads to the negative health and social effects mentioned above. The remedy they propose is simple: greater income redistribution.

There are at least three problems with their argument and the way they built up to it. We want to make clear that, for us, economic or income inequality is too easily and too generously pointed at as the sole cause behind health and well-being problems in nations, states and cities.

Omitted variables and overattribution

First, it is important to look closer at the statistical methods that are used: bivariate correlations (see Figure 4.1). Various reviewers have scrutinised choices made *within* the chosen method (e.g. Saunders, 2010; Snowdon, 2010; Rowlingson, 2011). They questioned the presence and strength of these associations by focusing on the choice of countries or US states that Wilkinson and Pickett (2009) left in or took out, the impact of particular outliers on the regression line, the linearity of the relationships, the appropriateness of a static (cross-sectional) perspective on income inequality in comparison with a dynamic one (by panel data), the robustness of the chosen measures, and so on. These are important and valid points, but we seek to illuminate the choice of the method, bivariate statistics, itself. Only including one independent variable clearly runs the risk of omitted variables and as a result of overattribution of health and social effects to economic inequality (Leigh, Jencks, & Smeeding, 2009, p. 486). This is known as 'omitted variable bias'.

In the case of health and well-being problems, omitted variables that could have had an impact are genetics (e.g. race), dietary patterns (sushi in Japan versus hamburgers in the United States), but also national–cultural factors (e.g. class divisions and relations) and governmental regimes or welfare models (Muntaner & Lynch, 1999; Leigh et al., 2009; Saunders, 2010; Rowlingson, 2011; de Vos, 2015). Hu, van Lenthe and Mackenbach (2015) do indeed show that all significant associations between income inequality in a country (as indicated by the Gini coefficient) on the on hand and different mortality indicators on the other, disappear when all other nation-specific effects are controlled for (through the use of nation 'fixed effects' and time-varying characteristics).

In a rebuttal to the critics (e.g. Saunders, 2010) who have raised this issue, Wilkinson and Pickett explain they did not include other factors because they wanted to keep it simple – you should not control for factors which form part of the causal chain' as those 'could remove the association between income inequality and health' and it 'would simply create unnecessary "noise"' (p. 285). But, considering any factor that reduces or eliminates a statistically significant relation between the two variables of interest is crucial – not just disturbing – for a good understanding of the complex and intricate causal relations behind national differences in the health and social phenomena that are under investigation. This is essential for coming up with effective policy measures to address these issues.

Relative or absolute poverty

One of the key factors that could (or should) have been controlled for, in addition, is the levels of deprivation within the investigated countries and the US states, to make sure that the effects found by Wilkinson and Pickett do not follow from differences in (absolute) poverty instead of inequality (see Chapter 1 for the difference).[2] Especially because they claim that:

> these are not differences between high- and low-risk groups within populations which might apply only to a small portion of the population, or just to the poor. Rather, they are differences between the prevalence of different problems which apply to whole populations. (Wilkinson & Pickett, 2009, p. 173).

Therefore, the question should be: is there an *additional* negative effect of income or wealth inequality on top of people's income or wealth levels? In other words, are the poor extra unhealthy, extra violent, extra less educated and so on, because, on top of the fact that they are poor, others are richer? And conversely, are the rich unhealthier, more violent, less educated because others are poorer?

Testing this would require a multilevel regression analysis in which both the effect of (absolute) income at the individual level and the relative income distribution (i.e. inequality) at the territorial (e.g. national) level are included (see Rowlingson, 2011, p. 20). Lynch et al. (2004) have carried out a meta-analysis of 98 aggregate and multilevel studies, and have come to the conclusion that the empirical support for an *additional* effect of income inequality above income levels is limited, let alone for a sizable effect[3] (Lynch et al., 2004, p. 5; see also Leigh et al., 2009, p. 487).

The issue of causality

Throughout the book by Wilkinson and Pickett (2009), they do not only show a *statistical* relation between income inequality and health and social problems, but they go one step further by implying, and sometimes explicitly claiming, a *causal* relation: 'inequality actually leads to poorer health *because* it is socially divisive' (p. 285; emphasis in original).

But what if income inequality and the dependent variable are *both* dependent upon some third variable, such as ethnic discrimination? It may well be that it is not the difference in income that causes the status anxiety and social stress as assumed by Wilkinson and Pickett, but the discrimination on the basis of ethnicity, which is at the same time also the source of income inequality (e.g. Leigh et al., 2009; Saunders, 2010). Then, redistributing income while leaving ethnic discrimination intact does not target the root of the problem.

The problematic logic becomes clearer when we look more closely at the corollary of the assumed causal relation and the solution that Wilkinson and Pickett put forward (p. 184). They assume that reducing economic inequality by means of redistribution (e.g. through taxes or benefits) improves health and social well-being of *all* groups in society, also of the rich. But redistribution leads to less income and wealth for the rich, which means they can spend less money, for instance, on health care and education. We believe it is hard to sustain that this will make the rich less violent, better educated and so on.

Finally, there may be the issue of 'reversed causality,' even though, in the case of health, not much evidence of that is found either (Leigh et al. 2009). A telling example in which reversed causality seems likely, again from a logical point of view, is social cohesion or social capital. Wilkinson and Pickett (2009) consider social capital to be a function of income inequality and measure it through the level of trust people have in the *other*.[4] However, the reverse is more likely:

> Sweden and Japan, for example, have the income distributions they have because of the kinds of societies they are. They are not cohesive societies because their incomes are equally distributed; their incomes are equally distributed because they evolved as remarkably cohesive societies (Saunders, 2010, p. 8).

In summary, the logical and empirical support for the negative (and positive) effects of economic inequality on the hand and economic growth, health and social well-being on the other is ambiguous.

The negative impact of economic segregation

Segregation, and economic segregation more specifically, is often assumed to have additional effects on individuals: so-called neighbourhood effects. Living in rich neighbourhoods is associated with positive effects on individual outcomes, and living in poor neighbourhoods with negative effects. In the literature, most attention has been given to the negative effects of segregation on people living in poor neighbourhoods. This will also be the main focus of this section.

Neighbourhood effects stemming from segregation have been a well-studied phenomenon in a wide range of scientific disciplines (from sociology to epidemiology, and from geography to economics) for many decades (see, for example, Gans 1961). After the book *The Truly Disadvantaged* by William Julius Wilson (1987), who, among other things, discusses the impact of selective outmigration and economic change on the emergence of neighbourhoods with a high concentration of poor and unemployed (Afro-American) people and subsequent effects this has on individuals living in these neighbourhoods, research on neighbourhood effects has taken off rapidly. According to van Ham, Manley, Bailey, (2012), more than 17,000 papers, books and (scientific) reports on (or at least mentioning) the words 'neighbourhood effects' have been published between the moment Wilson published his book in 1987 and the year 2010. We are well aware that a full overview of the literature is beyond the scope of this section, and, as such, we do not intend to provide such an overview (which seems an overambitious goal in general). Rather, we aim to discuss the main effects that are generally associated with economic segregation and the methodological issues that come with the actual measurement of the presence and size of these effects.

Mechanisms underlying neighbourhood effects

Neighbourhood effects occur if there is an *additional* effect of the neighbourhood characteristics on individual outcomes living in that neighbourhood. The key premise – of the concept of neighbourhood effects stemming from economic segregation – is the idea that, *ceteris paribus*, people are worse off living in a poor neighbourhood than in a rich neighbourhood as a result of the effect of a high concentration of poor people on individual outcomes (Cheshire, 2007). These outcomes may range from economic outcomes (e.g. income, labor market position) to school achievements of children, criminal behavior, or health status.

As Figure 4.2 illustrates, the composition of a neighbourhood's population (either by income or wealth or by any other characteristic) does not directly affect the outcomes of individuals living in these neighbourhoods; it does so through different mechanisms. Galster (2012), among others (e.g. Cheshire, 2007; Boschman, 2015), provides an overview of (the literature on) the various possible mechanisms that cause neighbourhood effects in general. He distinguishes between 16 different mechanisms that are grouped into four different categories: *social-mechanisms* (e.g. peer group effects, social networks); *institutional mechanisms* (e.g. lack of local institutional resources); *environmental mechanisms* (e.g. exposure to violence, crime, noise and pollution); and *geographical mechanisms* (e.g. a spatial mismatch due to a lack of good infrastructure restricting accessibility to job opportunities).

As Figure 4.2 shows, we do not consider the latter two groups as mechanisms through which the composition of the neighborhood affects individual outcomes. While we acknowledge that environmental and geographical mechanisms can negatively affect individual outcomes (economic), segregation is not the underlying cause of these neighbourhood effects (Cheshire, 2007).[5] Although the spatial concentration of people with low incomes often coincides with a spatial concentration of (people with) social problems, criminality and less well-developed physical characteristics of neighbourhoods, those characteristics are

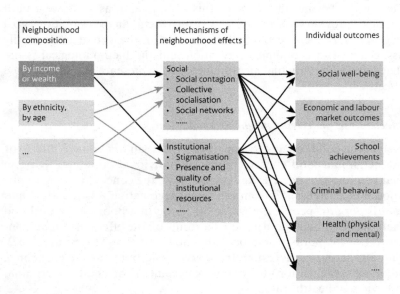

Figure 4.2 Neighbourhood effects of (economic) segregation.

not necessarily causally related.[6] Furthermore, rich neighbourhoods may also have high levels of crime (the wealth of its inhabitants may attract burglars) or less well-developed infrastructure (e.g. limited access to public transport).

Similarly to the way the neighbourhood's population is composed by income and wealth, other composition characteristics (e.g. ethnic background) may lead to neighbourhood effects as well. As these do not stem directly from processes of economic segregation, we will not discuss them further here, although we are aware of the fact that, in reality, those characteristics of a neighbourhood's composition coincide and may thus influence individual outcomes simultaneously.

Social mechanisms

The main social mechanisms through which the neighborhood composition may affect individual outcomes include, according to Galster (2012), social contagion, collective socialisation, and social networks. Social contagion refers to the possibility that one's attitude, behaviuor, and ambitions can be influenced by contact with peers such as your neighbors. Collective socialisation is related to this and refers to the presence of specific local social norms in neighbourhoods, often expressed by 'bad' or 'good' role models. This may take the form of neighbourhoods where working hard or studying hard is considered the norm, and neighbourhoods where being unemployed is the norm. If poor and rich neighbourhoods (because of the concentration of poor and rich people) differ in social norms and values, and this influences individual behavior in a positive or negative way; two identical persons living in different neighbourhoods may end up with different individual (economic) outcomes.

However, these social mechanisms may, in a similar way, lead to a positive effect of economic segregation in poor neighbourhoods as well. This is related to the idea that living in a neighbourhood with people with similar levels of income and wealth may lower the (psychological) effect of economic inequality in society as a whole (Galster, 2012). Wilkinson and Pickett (2009, p. 168) refer to this as a 'group density effect'. People in the lower levels of an income and wealth distribution may feel more comfortable if they live in neighbourhoods where the majority has the same socioeconomic position rather than living in areas where most inhabitants belong to the higher levels of income and wealth distribution (and *vice versa*) (see, e.g. Luttmer, 2005).

In addition, positive effects may arise due to social networks. Social networks refer to networks of interpersonal interaction. A concentration of people with similar socioeconomic characteristics may increase the likelihood of social interaction and informal networks between people (see Gans, 1961). As such, economic segregation may lead to a higher level of social cohesion in neighborhoods due to more commonalities in social-economic characteristics; as we discuss in Chapter 2, people prefer to have contact with people similar to themselves (Putnam, 2007). A high level of social cohesion in a neighborhood may increase the well-being of people. This is related to the notion that ethnic segregation may provide advantages for new migrants in a city, as neighborhoods with a high concentration of people with a similar background may function as a social safety net by providing informal support and information (van der Laan Bouma-Doff, 2007).

However, social networks may also lead to negative effects. Research on social networks and social capital (e.g. Lin, Ensel, & Vaughn, 1981; Mouw, 2006; Lin & Ao, 2008) suggests that the diversity and the socio-economic characteristics of an individual social network influence the labor market position of individuals (e.g. the chance of the unemployed to find a job; e.g. Sprengers et al., 1988). Neighborhoods may provide the spatial level where social networks are (partly) formed. If that is the case, economic segregation may lead to structural differences in the diversity of social networks between similar individuals living in poor or rich neighbourhoods. This, in turn, may lead to structural differences in information on, for instance, job opportunities and, consequently, to differences in individual economic outcomes.

Institutional mechanisms

The institutional mechanisms of neighborhood effects refer to the effects of decisions and actions of people and organisations outside the neighborhood that impact individuals in the neighbourhood. Economic segregation may lead, for instance, to negative images of neighbourhoods with a concentration of people with a low income (especially if this is combined with a concentration of social problems as well). Stigmatisation may lead to a lower chance of getting a job for someone living in such a neighbourhood in comparison to an otherwise equal person living in a richer neighbourhood if employers (implicitly or explicitly) weigh the neighbourhood as one of the criteria to assess a job candidate.

The presence and quality of institutional resources such as childcare facilities or the quality of schools may differ between rich and poor neighbourhoods if, for instance, highly qualified teachers have a preference to work in richer neighbourhoods. This may lead to differences in labour market opportunities between two otherwise identical persons as a result of living and growing up in different neighbourhoods.

In addition, stigmatisation may lead to a lower willingness to invest in these neighborhoods. This lower willingness to invest may range from public transport companies that decide to cut or downsize on specific lines, or banks less willing to supply mortgages in specific neighbourhoods (so-called redlining; e.g. Aalbers, 2006; Chapter 5).

Identification of neighbourhood effects

A crucial issue in the discussion on the negative impact of economic segregation through neighborhood effects is the proper identification of the mere presence and size of these effects. The key question is if there is indeed an *additional*, independent effect of neighbourhood characteristics, such as the share of low incomes on individual outcomes on top of individual characteristics. Or do these neighbourhood characteristics simply reflect the fact that people with a low income tend to live in the same neighbourhoods (sorting), rather than actually causing these lower incomes? To put it along the lines of Cheshire (2007), do poor neighbourhoods make people poor, or do poor people live in unattractive neighbourhoods because they cannot afford to live elsewhere? To what extent can the chance of someone having a low income or being unemployed be attributed to characteristics of the individual person, and to what extent is this also the result of the fact that they are living near other people without a job or with a low income?

A wide range of empirical studies tries to disentangle possible neighbourhood effects from the effects of other factors, such as education or household and even family characteristics, by advanced statistical and econometric techniques (see Durlauf, 2004; Hedman & van Ham, 2012, among others, for an overview). The idea is to see if, after taking into account a wide range of individual characteristics (and perhaps regional characteristics), there are significant differences between people in, for instance, income or unemployment in poor and rich neighbourhoods. If these differences are indeed statistically significantly different from zero, it is likely that neighbourhood effects are present, since the impact of individual characteristics is controlled; at least conceptually, the only differences between the persons is the neighbourhood.

The results of these studies (see, e.g. van Ham et al., 2012 for an overview) vary; in many studies, there are indications of (small) neighbourhood effects of economic segregation (e.g. Galster, Andersson, Musterd, & Kauppinen, 2008), yet, in other cases, no such effect can be found (e.g. Bolster et al., 2007). For those studies that do find an indication of neighbourhood effects, the relative size of these effects is much smaller than the relative size of factors at the individual level (e.g. the level of education has a much stronger effect on an individual's chance of employment than the characteristics of the neighbourhood). In addition to this, several studies show that the size or impact of neighbourhood effects differ between specific subgroups of the population of a neighbourhood (e.g. van der Klaauw & van Ours, 2003; Miltenburg & van de Werfhorst, 2017). Yet other studies (see Galster, 2012 for an overview) find nonlinear relations between neighborhood characteristics and individual outcomes, suggesting that there may be critical thresholds before neighbourhood effects occur.

According to Nieuwenhuis (2016), who performed a meta-analysis of 88 empirical studies on neighbourhood effects, there may be a publication bias in studies that suggest the presence of neighbourhood effects. He finds an unlikely high share[7] of studies that estimate a statistically significant effect compared to the ones that find an insignificant effect. This suggests that studies that do find a (significant) effect of neighbourhood characteristics are more likely to be published than studies that do not find such an effect. This is a very common methodological problem identified in the meta-analysis literature (e.g. de Dominicis, Florax, & de Groot, 2008).

Altogether, this leads to the suggestion that there is no compelling evidence of and consensus on the mere presence of neighbourhood effects in general, let alone on the size of them. As Cheshire (2007, p. 2) puts it: 'there is surprisingly little evidence that living in poor neighbourhoods makes people poorer and erodes their life chances, independently of those factors that contribute to their poverty in the first place'.

One of the reasons for this mixed evidence is the fact that several empirical issues make it highly difficult to disentangle individual effects from neighbourhood effects. Similar to studies on the effects of economic inequality, many empirical studies on the effect of economic segregation suffer from 'omitted variable bias': not all relevant individual characteristics can always be measured. This may result from a lack of data availability, but, sometimes, relevant factors, such as differences in talent (beyond formal education) and motivation (see also Chapter 2), are simply very difficult (if not impossible) to measure in a proper way (as pointed out, for instance, by Boschman, 2015 in the introduction to her book). These differences affect economic segregation as they may lead to differences in income and, consequently, opportunities in the housing market. As a corollary, it is very likely that two people with similar measurable characteristics, such as education, but different talents or motivation, end up living in different neighbourhoods, which is called a selection effect (see, e.g. Cheshire, 2007; Hedman & van Ham, 2012).

This is an important issue, as van Ham and Manley (2013) argue that selection effects are often not properly taken into account, leading to incorrect conclusions: 'we suggest that many studies claiming to have found evidence of neighbourhood effects only found selection effects' (p. 10). In a research setting where formal education is properly controlled for but other 'hard-to-measure' variables are not, differences between income for both persons may, therefore, be incorrectly attributed to neighbourhood effects, which leads to an overestimation of the negative economic effects of neighbourhoods (and, indirectly, of economic segregation).[8]

To tackle this problem, increasingly, studies use data that track moving and non-moving people for several years and use advanced econometric techniques (such as panel data analysis or propensity matching) to control for unobserved differences between individuals (e.g. Sharkey, 2012). Other studies try to tackle this issue by using data that are based on or resemble 'natural experiments' (Kling, Liebman, & Katz, 2007), such as the *Moving to Opportunity* project in the United States, where people from poor neighbourhoods were assigned vouchers enabling them to move to better neighbourhoods (see, e.g. Small & Feldman, 2012).

According to Durlauf (2004), empirical studies based on data from these 'quasi-experiments' find no to little impact of neighbourhoods on economic outcome variables, as opposed to studies based on non-experimental observational data, which often do find significant neighbourhood effects with, on average, a higher impact. However, more recent studies (see Chapter 1 of van Ham et al., 2012 for an overview) using data from the *Moving to Opportunity* project do find significant neighbourhood effects, for instance, on the future income of children who moved to better neighbourhoods (Chetty, Hendren, & Katz, 2016).

Altogether, research on the size and presence of neighbourhood effects is broad and increasing. As methodological techniques and data availability improve, neighbourhood effects and selection effects can increasingly be disentangled. This does not imply that, up to now, there has been a clear consensus on the presence of neighbourhood effects. Given the current state of knowledge, it seems fair to conclude that economic segregation through neighbourhood effects may lead to a negative impact on individual (socio-economic) outcome. However, this is not the case for all neighbourhoods with a concentration of lower incomes, and not necessarily for all people in these neighbourhoods. Moreover, if these effects are present, the relative impact is generally limited when compared to individual characteristics such as talent.

From individual effects to city level effects

Economic segregation can – mainly through social-interactive and institutional mechanisms – have negative consequences in the form of neighbourhood effects on individual socio-economic outcomes. Although this is problematic in itself for people living in poor neighbourhoods, this can also, at least conceptually, have a negative impact on the city as a whole, both from an economic and a social point of view.

From an economic point of view, the presence of neighbourhood effects is a prime example of negative externalities or market failures: people have a disadvantage in, for instance, the labour market (higher chance of being without a job, having a lower income and wealth) for reasons caused by others. This leads to a welfare loss at the city level for both the people living in poor neighbourhoods and, for instance, the companies that may suffer from a suboptimal supply of potential employees.[9] Moreover, if economic segregation generates neighbourhood effects that negatively influence income and wealth levels of individuals, higher levels of economic segregation will lead to a higher level of economic inequality at the level of cities as well (and the possible negative effects of economic inequality will increase as well; see section 'The negative impact of economic inequality').

In addition, from a social point of view, the concentration of lower income households in combination with different social problems in low-income neighbourhoods may lead to a negative spiral where some neighbourhoods will offer a quality of life to their inhabitants that is below the socially acceptable minimum. This may have negative effects on the outcomes of individuals living in these neighbourhoods, but it may also lead to a feeling of being neglected or ignored by the rest of the city. This, in turn, may lead to social unrest within these neighbourhoods, as was suggested to be the case in Paris, London, and Stockholm (e.g. Tammaru, Marcińczak, van Ham, & Musterd, 2016).

Although there are possible advantages of economic segregation with regard to social cohesion, they refer to the advantages for the segregated group itself. This advantage may be considered an advantage for society or the city as well, but could also be a disadvantage at this aggregated level. Economic segregation may lead to higher levels of social cohesion or trust at the level of the segregated groups, but, at the same time, may lower social cohesion and trust between members of the different groups. This is the case if, as a result of segregation and high levels of social cohesion between segregated groups, these groups are increasingly 'living apart together' within cities. As quoted from *The Guardian* in Chapter 1: 'Londoners of different means live utterly separate lives' (The Observer View on London's Wealth Gap, 2015). This could lead to a polarised society, which is, by some, ultimately associated with an erosion of the basis for a democratic society (see, e.g. Massey, 1996; Tammaru et al., 2016). The question of whether this polarisation is indeed resulting (to a large extent) from segregation is, however, open for debate and an empirical question to be answered.

Notes

1 The principle of decreasing returns is the decrease of (marginal) return on each added production factor (capital in this case), with all other production factors remaining constant.
2 Chapter 2 of *The Spirit Level* is called 'Poverty or Inequality,' but, in the chapter, poverty refers to overall wealth (GDP) levels in the countries and states included in the analysis, not the share of the population below a social minimum or poverty threshold (absolute poverty).
3 Similarly, the literature on happiness, as indicated by 'life satisfaction', also reports mixed and ambiguous results (Helliwell, Layard, & Sachs, 2012, pp. 70–71).
4 Wilkinson and Pickett (2009) use only one indicator of social cohesion or capital: trust. Other factors are left out. Saunders (2010) shows that there is no relationship between income inequality on the one hand, and other proxies for cohesion, such as racial tolerance and voluntary memberships, on the other.
5 Although one could think of a situation where decisions on public transport investments and divestments influencing the accessibility of neighbourhoods are influenced by the income levels of neighbourhoods.
6 There are many studies that focus on these types of neighborhood effects. Based on an overview of a wide range of empirical studies, Galster (2012), Tampubolon (2012), among others concluded that the evidence for the presence of these types of neighbourhood effects is mixed.
7 Around the arbitrary boundary for statistical significance (based on a *p*-value of .05).
8 A counterargument may be that exactly these differences in motivation could be the result of differences in neighbourhood characteristics. This may indeed be the case, but this does not alter the conclusion that, even with advanced econometric techniques, it is impossible to pinpoint the presence and magnitude of neighbourhood effects if one suffers from an omitted variable bias.
9 One can discuss whether the presence of positive neighbourhood effects in rich neighbourhoods leading to additional positive effects for people living in these neighbourhoods may balance the negative impact of negative neighbourhood effects at the level of a city as a whole.

References

Aalbers, M. B. (2006). *Who's Afraid of Red, Yellow and Green? Geographies of Redlining and Exclusion in the Netherlands and Italy*. Amsterdam, the Netherlands: University of Amsterdam.

Aghion, P., Caroli, E., & García-Peñalosa, C. (1999). Inequality and economic growth: The perspective of the new growth theories. *Journal of Economic Literature, 37*(4), 1615–1660.

Bolster, A., Burgess, S., Johnston, R., Jones, K., Propper, C., & Starker, R. (2007). Neighbourhoods, households and income dynamics: A semi-parametric investigation of neighbourhood effects. *Journal of Economic Geography, 7*(1), 1–38.

Boschman, S. (2015). Selective mobility, segregation and neighbourhood effects. Delft, the Netherlands: Technical University of Delft.

Cheshire, P. (2007). *Segregated Neighbourhoods and Mixed Communities.* York, UK: Joseph Rowntree Foundation.

Chetty, R., Hendren, N., & Katz, L. F. (2016). The effects of exposure to better neighbourhoods on children: New evidence from the *Moving to Opportunity* experiment. *The American Economic Review, 106*(4), 855–902.

de Dominicis, L., Florax, R. J. G. M., & de Groot, H. L. F. (2008). A meta-analysis on the relationship between income inequality and economic growth. *Scottish Journal of Political Economy, 55*(5), 654–682.

de la Croix, D., & Doepke, M. (2003). Inequality and growth: Why differential fertility matters. *The American Economic Review, 93*(4), 1091–1113.

de Vos, M. (2015). Ongelijk maar fair. Waarom onze samenleving ongelijker is dan we vrezen, maar rechtvaardiger dan we hopen [Unequal but fair. Why our society is more unequal than we fear, but more fair than we hope for]. Tielt: the Netherlands: Uitgeverij LannooCampus.

Durlauf, S. N. (2004). Neighbourhood effects. In J. V. Henderson & J. F. Thisse (Eds.), *Handbook of Regional and Urban Economics* (Vol. 4, pp. 2173–2242). Amsterdam, the Netherlands: Elsevier.

Galster, G. C. (2012). The mechanism(s) of neighbourhood effects: Theory, evidence and policy implications. In M. van Ham, D. Manley, N. Bailey, L. Simpson, & D. Maclennan (Eds.), *Neighbourhood Effects Research: New Perspectives* (pp. 23–56). Dordrecht, the Netherlands: Springer.

Galster, G., Andersson, R., Musterd, S., & Kauppinen, T. M. (2008). Does neighbourhood income mix affect earnings of adults? New evidence from Sweden. *Journal of Urban Economics, 63*(3), 858–870.

Gans, H. (1961). The balanced community. Homogeneity or heterogeneity in residential areas. *Journal of the American Institute of Planners, 27*(3), 176–184.

Hedman, L., & van Ham, M. (2012). Understanding neighbourhood effects: Selection bias and residential mobility. In M. van Ham, D. Manley, N. Bailey, L. Simpson, & D. Maclennan (Eds.), *Neighbourhood effects research: New perspectives* (pp. 79–99). Dordrecht, the Netherlands: Springer.

Helliwell, J., Layard, R., & Sachs, J. (2012). *Word Happiness Report.* New York, NY: Sustainable Development Solutions Network.

Hu, Y., van Lenthe, F., & Mackenbach, J. P. (2015). Income inequality, life expectancy and cause-specific mortality in 43 European countries, 1987–2008: A fixed effects study. *European Journal of Epidemiology, 30*(8), 615–625.

Kling, J. R., Liebman, J. B., & Katz, L. F. (2007). Experimental analysis of neighbourhood effects. *Econometrica, 75*(1), 83–119.

Kuznets, S. (1995). Economic Growth and Income Inequality. *The American Economic Review, 45*(1), 1–28.

Leigh, A., Jencks, C., & Smeeding, T. M. (2009). Health and economic inequality. In W. Salverda, B. Nolan, & T. M. Smeeding (Eds.), *The Oxford Handbook of Economic Inequality* (pp. 384–405). Oxford, UK: Oxford University Press.

Lin, N., & Ao, D. (2008). The invisible hand of social capital: An exploratory study. In N. Lin & B. H. Erickson (Eds.), *Social Capital: An International Research Program* (pp. 107–132). New York, NY: Oxford University Press.

Lin, N., Ensel, W. M., & Vaughn, J. C. (1981). Social resources and strength of ties: Structural factors in occupational status attainment. *American Journal of Sociology, 46*(4), 393–405.

Luttmer, E. F. P. (2005). Neighbors as negatives: Relative earnings and well-being. *Quarterly Journal of Economics, 120*(3), 963–1002.

Lynch, J., Smith, G. D., Harper, S., Hillemeier, M., Ross, N., Kaplan, G. A., & Wolfson, M. (2004). Is income inequality a determinant of population health? Part 1: A systematic review. *Millbank Quarterly, 82*(1), 5–99.

Massey, D. S. (1996). The age of extremes: Concentrated affluence and poverty in the twenty-first century. *Demography, 33*(4), 395–412.

Miltenburg, E. M., & van de Werfhorst, H. G. (2017). Finding a job: The role of the neighbourhood for different household configurations over the life course. *European Sociological Review, 33*(1), 30–45.

Mouw, T. (2006). Estimating the causal effect of social capital: A review of recent research. *Annual Review of Sociology, 32*, 79–102.

Muntaner, C., & Lynch, J. (1999). Income inequality, social cohesion, and class relations: A critique of Wilkinson's neo-Durkheimian research program. *International Journal of Health Services, 29*(1), 59–81.

Nieuwenhuis, J. (2016). Publication bias in the neighbourhood effects literature. *Geoforum, 70*, 89–92.

Perotti, R. (1996). Growth, income distribution, and democracy: What the data say. *Journal of Economic Growth, 1*(2), 149–187.

Putnam, R. D. (2007). *E pluribus unum*: Diversity and community in the twenty-first century, the 2006 Johan Skytte Prize Lecture. *Scandinavian Political Studies, 30*(2), 137–174.

Rowlingson, K. (2011). *Does Income Inequality Cause Health and Social Problems?* London, UK: Joseph Rowntree Foundation.

Saunders, P. (2010). *Beware False Prophets: Equality, the Good Society, and The Spirit Level.* London, UK: Policy Exchange.

Sharkey, P. (2012). An alternative approach to addressing selection into and out of social settings: Neighborhood change and African American children's economic outcomes. *Sociological Methods and Research, 41*(2), 251–293.

Small, M., & Feldman, J. (2012). Ethnographic evidence, heterogeneity, and neighbourhood effects after moving to opportunity. In M. van Ham, D. Manley, N. Bailey, L. Simpson, & D. Maclennan (Eds.), *Neighbourhood*

Effects Research: New Perspectives (pp. 57–77). Dordrecht, the Netherlands: Springer.

Snowdon, C. J. (2010). *The Spirit Level Delusion: Fact-Checking the Left's New Theory of Everything*. Ripon, UK: Little Dice.

Sprengers, M., Tazelaar, F., & Flap, H. D. (1988). Social resources, situational constraints, and re-employment. *Netherlands Journal of Sociology*, *24*(2), 98–116.

Stiglitz, J. E. (2012). *The Price of Inequality: How Today's Divided Society Endangers Our Future*. New York, NY: W. W. Norton and Company.

Tammaru, T., Marcińczak, S., van Ham, M., & Musterd, S. (Eds.). (2016). *Socio-Economic Segregation in European Capital Cities*. London, UK: Routledge.

Tampubolon, G. (2012). Neighbourhood social capital and individual mental health. In M. van Ham, D. Manley, N. Bailey, L. Simpson, & D. Maclennan (Eds.), *Neighbourhood Effects Research: New Perspectives* (pp. 175–193). Dordrecht, the Netherlands: Springer.

The Observer View on London's Wealth Gap. (2015, March 8). *The Guardian*, https://www.theguardian.com/commentisfree/2015/mar/08/observer-view -on-london

Van der Klaauw, B., & van Ours, J. C. (2003). From welfare to work: Does the neighbourhood matter? *Journal of Public Economics*, *87*(5), 957–985.

Van der Laan Bouma-Doff, W. (2007). Confined contact: Residential segregation and ethnic bridges in the Netherlands. *Urban Studies*, *44*(5–6), 997–1017.

Van Ham, M., & Manley, D. (2013). Occupational mobility and living in deprived neighbourhoods: Housing tenure differences in "neighbourhood effects." IZA Discussion Paper No. 7815. Institute for the Study of Labor, http://ftp.iza.org/dp7815.pdf

Van Ham, M., Manley, D., Bailey, N., Simpson, L., & Maclennan, D. (Eds.). (2012). *Neighbourhood Effects Research: New Perspectives*. Dordrecht, the Netherlands: Springer.

Wilkinson, R., & Pickett, K. (2009). *The Spirit Level: Why Equality Is Better for Everyone*. London, UK: Penguin Books.

Wilson, W. J. (1987). *The Truly Disadvantaged: The Inner City, the Underclass, and Public Policy*. Chicago, IL: University of Chicago Press.

5 Reflecting on the moral implications[1]

> Apart perhaps from a few half-baked neo-Nietzscheans, every-one is in favor of justice. Equality, by contrast, seems only to be embraced unreservedly by political fanatics and philosophers.
>
> (Miller, 1997, pp. 223–224)

According to many, economic inequality is not only problematic if it has a negative impact on other social phenomena, as discussed in Chapter 4, but also when looked at *in and of itself*. In other words, when looked at not merely instrumentally, but also intrinsically. In this chapter, we reflect on the moral relevance of economic inequality and, alongside that, segregation. We reflect on the concepts of 'economic inequality and segregation', particularly on the relative nature of the two nouns 'inequality' and 'segregation'. Subsequently, we reflect on the material nature of the adjective 'economic'.

First, we distinguish between equality and justice (section 'Equality and distributive justice'). Second, we deal with the notion of 'distribution' (in 'distributive justice') and try to show how the implicit erroneous idea of a pie that must be sliced by someone or something and distributed over society has affected the discussion on economic inequality and segregation (section 'The pie metaphor'). Third, we try to refine the concept of (in)equality by distinguishing between different forms, such as 'good' and 'bad' inequality, and equality of outcomes and equality of opportunity (section 'Good and bad economic inequality'). We then emphasise the tension between aiming for greater economic equality and desegregation and equally (or more) important goals in liberal democratic societies: liberty and equality of rights (section 'The impracticability of aiming for economic equality'). After that, we reflect on the moral (ir)relevance of 'relative poverty' (i.e. economic inequality) in relation to the concept of 'absolute poverty' (section 'The same or enough? About the moral relevance of economic inequality'). Similarly, we reflect on relative *neighbourhood* poverty (i.e. segregation) versus absolute *neighbourhood* poverty (section 'The moral relevance of (economic) segregation'). We finalise this chapter by questioning the common preoccupation with material resources when *economic* inequality and segregation are discussed, and try to raise awareness for the importance of 'capabilities' (section 'Reflecting on the material dimension of *economic* inequality and segregation').

Equality and distributive justice

In the debate, economic inequality and segregation on the one hand and (social) injustice on the other, are often discussed as if there are the same. As we explained earlier, we consider economic inequality and segregation as empirical or descriptive concepts, since they refer to the skewness of an economic and spatial distribution, respectively. Justice is a normative or prescriptive concept: it deals with the principle of moral rightness.

In relation to inequality, we tend to speak about 'distributive justice': the principle of moral rightness regarding a distribution (of wealth, for instance). In the common view that we have taken as our starting point – 'urban-economic inequality and the spatial sorting thereof (that is, segregation) are increasing, this a bad thing and money and people (in the case of segregation) need to be redistributed in response' – many who judge inequality as 'bad' and call for redistribution, also judge inequality explicitly, or, more often, implicitly, from a perspective of 'egalitarian justice' (e.g. Wilkinson & Pickett, 2009; Dorling 2014; Piketty, 2014; Atkinson, 2015). 'Egalitarian justice' is a type of 'distributive justice' that has as its central principle that a distribution is right if everyone has an *equal* share or not too unequal a share: 'the more equal, the more just' (Smith 1994, p. 119). Consequently, a distribution that is unequal is considered unjust by those who equate equality with justice. In this chapter, we reflect on the moral soundness of the principle of 'egalitarian justice' and the conflation of equality and justice. We do this, for instance, by taking into consideration other principles of 'distributive justice,' such as Rawls's 'justice as fairness' (1971, 1993) and Nozick's 'entitlement theory of justice' (1974) (see the List of Concepts for definitions).[2]

Let us start with a noncontextualised thought experiment, as presented in Figure 5.1. What situation is to be preferred? In situation 1, person A has 10 coins, five times as many as person B, who has two coins. Situation 2 is more equal. Now, person A only has three times as many coins as person B. From an equality point of view, this second

Figure 5.1 Inequality experiment.

situation is preferable to situation 1, although person A now has fewer resources and the number of coins of person B has not increased. In situation 3, person A has only two coins left, while person B's number has been halved and is now down to one. What is the most just situation? Those who endorse the notion of 'egalitarian justice' would, consequently, prefer situation 3 over situations 1 and 2, despite the fact that not only person A but also person B is worse off in that situation.

The pie metaphor

One reason why economic inequality is debated so heavily, and why those who are in favour of equality of material distributions prefer situation 3 over situations 1 and 2 (Figure 5.1), may have to do with the often implicitly present pie metaphor. It literally means that an income distribution is considered to be the result of someone or something cutting and dividing a pie. This is mistaken for two reasons, the first being the (implicit) false assumption that there is a central entity slicing and distributing a pie:

> Hearing the term 'distribution,' most people presume that some thing or mechanism uses some principle or criterion to give out a supply of things. Into this process of distributing shares some error may have crept .... [However,] there is no *central* distribution, no person or group entitled to control all the resources, jointly deciding how they are to be doled out. (Nozick 1974, p. 149, emphasis in original)

Of course, there are central entities (i.e. states) that affect income and wealth distributions through pre- and redistributive measures, but that is something else than holding all resources and handing them out.

The second is the assumption of a zero-sum game – of a supply, a pie – with a *fixed* size. In that case, the size of one piece is, inevitably, at the expense of another. In other words, if I get a bigger piece, others would have to settle for less and *vice versa*. However, the fact is that economic development in general, and urban economic development in particular, is not a zero-sum game (de Vos, 2015; Martin, Pike, Tyler, & Gardiner, 2015; Thissen, de Graaff, & van Oort, 2016). A person may improve his income, an organisation its profit, and a city its economy without it having an adverse effect on the income, profit, or economy of that of others. If your salary goes up, your colleagues' salary usually does not go down. Rather, the overall wage expenses of the company or the public agency go up. The same goes for countries: the gross domestic product (GDP) is not fixed; it is even quite volatile. Between 2010 and 2015, the US GDP went up from nearly 15,000 billion dollars to nearly 18,000 billion dollars.[3] In other words, the entire pie grows and its size is not, *a priori*, fixed.

In the literature on regional-economic growth and competition, this is illustrated by the distinction between 'demand-led growth' and 'structural growth,' as depicted in Figure 5.2. Demand-led growth is growth of a region through an increase of the demand for goods in its (export) sales markets. As a result of demand-led growth, the economy of the region grows independently from, and not at the expense of, other regions. If growth of the region occurs because it manages to

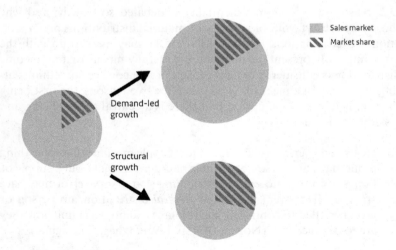

Figure 5.2 Economic growth and market shares.
Source: Thissen, M., de Graaff, T., & van Oort, F. G., 2016.

improve its competitive advantage over other regions, and increase its market share on its sales markets at the expense of these competing regions, it is called structural growth. Roughly 75 per cent of regional growth in Europe is demand-led, and only 25 per cent is structural (Thissen et al., 2016).

The same applies to people: when they improve their wealth, they do so primarily because of a growing market in which they participate, such as, for instance, the new knowledge-intensive economy in the San Fancisco Bay Area or Greater Boston (e.g. Moretti, 2012). Those jobs, and the income that is derived from them, often emerge independently from and in addition to, and not at the expense of, the jobs and income of others. That said, there *is* always some competition, and people's jobs may become redundant because of other people or machines with a competitive advantage[4] (see Chapter 2).

Despite the the non-fixity of a distribution – the fact that growth of one is not necessarily at the expense of the other – and the fact that a central distributor is absent may sound self-evident, it is not the way income distribution is commonly discussed. This may explain why the coverage of high or increasing inequality evokes such strong emotions and calls for action.

Good and bad economic inequality

It is important to emphasise that not all types of economic inequality are equally good or bad and relevant from a moral perspective. In a beautifully written – unfortunately in Dutch, as it deserves a bigger audience – and researched book that translates as *Unequal but Fair*, Belgian philosopher and economist Marc de Vos distinguishes between 'good' and 'bad' inequality (2015, pp. 23–24).

'Bad' inequality he considers to be the result of inequality of opportunities. There are obvious differences in talent, de Vos (2015) says, which we cannot but accept. Not accepting them would be the same as not accepting nature (see Chapter 2). But, given that fact, everyone should be able to use their talent maximally, and equal opportunities should, therefore, be created for all. Equality of opportunities must be considered broader than equality of (formal/legal) rights (see section 'The impracticability of aiming for economic equality' for a discussion of those).[5] In his book *Injustice*, Dorling (2010) focuses on several factors, such as elitism, social exclusion and prejudice, through which the ideal of equal opportunities is thwarted. Creating opportunities for all is not an easy agenda; it is costly and may never be fully achieved, as we will never be able to eradicate privileges, prejudices and unfair treatment entirely. It is, however, an important aim to strive for an equality that enables everyone to fulfil their potential to the fullest (de Vos, 2015, pp. 23–24).

'Good' inequality is inequality in material outcomes (for instance, income) that is the result of the free, unequal realisation of unequal human potential. Unequal outcomes are an *inevitable* consequence of equal opportunities. According to de Vos, this is not just inevitable, it is good, too: in a society that does its job well, material inequality is the *success* of equal opportunities for unequal talents and unequal preferences (2015, p. 24).

It must be noted that, over time, good inequality may lead to bad inequality: 'where there are greater inequalities of outcome, equal opportunity is a significantly more distant prospect' (Wilkinson & Pickett, 2009, p. 169). Differences in intergenerational accumulation of capital may lead to differences in opportunities (Corak, 2013; van Ham et al., 2014).

The currency of equality of opportunity

There is much debate in the philosophical literature about the *currency*, or indicator, of equality in general and of equality of opportunity in particular (Dworkin, 1981a; 1981b; Arneson, 1989; Cohen, 1989; Radcliffe-Richards, 1997; Wolff, 2007). Arneson (1989, p.86), to discuss just one, beseeches us to focus on 'equal opportunity for welfare,' which implies that 'all people face effectively equivalent arrays of options'. This compensates for circumstances and lack of abilities that prevent people from choosing particular options if they wish to and happen to be aware of them. After creating these 'equivalent arrays of options,' any inequality in welfare lies within each individual's control. The concept of 'equal opportunity for welfare' comes close to Amartya Sen's emphasis on the (equal) possession of *capabilities* (1983, 2009),[6] to which we come back in the last section of this chapter.

Much of the discussion seems to centre around the distinction between what simply happens to us and over which we have no control ('brute luck') and what we choose or allow to happen to us ('option luck'). In case of the latter, choices result, for instance, from expensive preferences or tastes and bad judgments.[7] What is innate or uncontrollable and what is the result of conscious decisions and personal responsibility? In addition, the discussion is about the type of luck inequality that renders compensating actions (if any[8]). These are very difficult choices to make and difficult questions to answer, and they go beyond what we can do in the context of this short book. However, what we can say is that the moral discussion on equality is much more complicated than the common focus on equality of material distributions (i.e. economic inequality) and the redistribution to bring about that ideal. However, we continue in line with this common focus on economic inequality (and segregation).

The impracticability of aiming for economic equality

We argued that there is 'good' inequality next to 'bad' inequality, and that the pie metaphor often blocks our view to appreciate this distinction. Besides, striving for material equality is also hard to achieve. Moroni (2013, pp. 67–69, 2015) raises two problems or conflicts that we meet when we aim for total or greater economic equality within the context of liberal-democratic countries: (1) formal equality (i.e., equality of rights) is incompatible with economic equality, and (2) liberty upsets patterns such as equal material distributions.

Incompatibility of economic equality and formal equality

Liberal philosophers have pointed at the incompatibility of material equality and formal equality (i.e. equality of rights). Formal equality is the first principle of 'justice as fairness' as formulated by John Rawls: 'each person is to have an equal right to the most extensive basic liberty compatible with a similar liberty for others' (1971, p. 60). Most of us subscribe to the idea of equal rights as a cornerstone of liberal democratic societies. What is often overlooked, is that equal rights lead to unequal distributions of income and wealth (as the next paragraph will show). Redistributing income and wealth to reduce inequalities and aiming for economic equality logically implies the reduction or expropriation of rights of those whose money is recouped for redistribution to those who have less (Hayek, 1944; Nozick, 1974; Moroni, 2013, 2015). The result is formal inequality. As a matter of fact (or logic), this is correct. Whether it is immoral is a different discussion. Empirically, we know that different countries make different trade-offs between formal equality and material equality.

The logic also applies to segregation. If the distributional pattern is deemed undesirable, or, more specifically, if a city is considered too segregated, it would require reducing or eliminating rights for some people to settle freely, move freely and to trade homes to correct that distributional pattern. It, too, would lead to formal inequality.

Liberty upsets economic equality and desegregation

The second reason why an equal distribution is hard to obtain has to do with the liberties that people have in liberal- democratic countries. If you grant people a certain degree of liberty, (desired) patterns, such as material equality, are very unlikely to occur: liberty upsets patterns, as Robert Nozick claims (1974, pp. 160–164). To support his argument, Nozick uses a thought experiment, in which Wilt Chamberlain, a famous NBA basketball player from the 1960s and 1970s, plays a key role. Nozick starts with distribution D1, in which everyone has an equal share or any other share of choice. Then he constructs the following storyline:

> Now suppose Wilt Chamberlain is greatly in demand by basketball teams, being a great gate attraction. (Also suppose contracts run only for a year, with players being free agents.) He signs the following sort of contract with a team: In each home game, twenty-five cents from the price of each ticket of admission goes to him. (We ignore the question of whether he is "gouging" the owners, letting them look out for themselves.) The season starts, and people cheerfully attend his team's games; they buy their tickets, each time dropping a separate twenty-five cents of the admission price into a special box with Chamberlain's name on it. They are excited about seeing him play; it is worth the total admission to them. Let us suppose that in one season one million persons attend his home games, and Wilt Chamberlain winds up with $250,000, a much larger sum than the average income and larger even than anyone else has. Is he entitled to his income? Is this new distribution D2, unjust? If so, why? There is *no* question about whether each of these people was entitled control over the resources they held in D1, because that was the distribution (your favorite) that (for the purposes of the argument) we assumed was acceptable. Each of these persons *chose* to give twenty-five cents of their money to Chamberlain. They could have spent it on going to the movies, or on candy bars, or on copies of *Dissent* magazine, or of *Monthly Review*. But they all, at least one million of them, converged on giving it to Wilt Chamberlain in exchange for watching him play basketball. If D1 was a just distribution, and people voluntarily moved from it to D2, transferring parts of their shares they were given under D1 (what was it for if not to do something with?), isn't D2 also just? If the people were entitled to dispose of the resources to which they were entitled (under D1), didn't this include their being entitled to give it to, or exchange it with, Wilt Chamberlain? Can anyone else complain on

grounds of justice? Each person already has his legitimate share under D1. Under D1, there is nothing that anyone has that anyone else has a claim of justice against. After someone transfers something to Wilt Chamberlain, third parties *still* have their legitimate shares; *their* shares are not changed. (Nozick, 1974, p. 161; emphasis in original)

We use this extensive quote to illustrate the conflict between liberty and (distributional) patterns such as equality. Material or economic equality are highly unlikely and, at best, accidental and temporary events, when people have property rights, the freedom to trade and are not disadvantaged by freedom-encroaching behaviour such as fraud, enslavement, theft and monopolisitic rent-seeking. To us that seems quite irrefutable.[9] In addition, we believe it is equally applicable to the issue of segregation. If you grant people the freedom to settle where they want, to move homes and to trade homes (in the case of owner-occupiers), chances are slim that people from different socio-economic groups will spread evenly over cities, especially because of sorting processes due to people's preference to live with like-minded people (see Chapter 2).

The same or enough? About the moral relevance of economic inequality

One may say that 'good' economic inequality is not morally unjust – and is even desirable economically– or that economic equality is impracticable because it contradicts liberty and formal equality. One may even go further by questioning the relevance of one having more or less than the other. Nobel laureate Amartya Sen has argued that:

The fact that some people have a lower standard of living than others is certainly proof of inequality, but by itself it cannot be a proof of poverty unless we know something more about the standard of living that these people do in fact enjoy. (Sen 1983, p. 159)

The thought experiment that we showed in Figure 5.1, of course, does not tell us whether the number of coins persons A and B possess are *enough* to stay alive, live a decent life or maintain a minimum standard of living that we think suitable. If we assume that having one coin is not enough to meet the minimally acceptable standard of living, person B lives below that minimum standard in situation 3, as Figure 5.3 indicates. The fact that, in situation 3, persons A and B are relatively equal, compared to situation 1 and 2, does not help person B (nor person A) at all. However, many scholars who are active in the

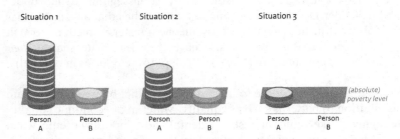

Figure 5.3 Inequality and (absolute) poverty experiment.

debate on inequality seem to focus more on the extent to which the rich have more than others – especially those who focus on the top 1 per cent of the income distribution (e.g. Dorling, 2014) – than whether the poor have what they need. 'We care ethically only about the Gini coefficient, not the *condition* of the working class,' according to McCloskey (2014, emphasis added).

Therefore, it may be said that economic inequality (Frankfurt, 1987; Moroni, 2013, pp. 74–75, 2015):

> … is not as such of particular moral importance. With respect to the distribution of economic assets, what is important from the point of view of morality is not that everyone should have *the same* but that each should have *enough*. If everyone had enough, it would be of no moral consequence whether some had more than others. (Frankfurt, 1987, p. 21, emphasis in original)

Here, 'enough' pertains to reaching a *standard*, not to reaching a *limit*. There is no moral objection to exceeding the sufficiency standard (Frankfurt 1987, p. 37). This is called "the doctrine of sufficiency," as opposed to "the doctrine of egalitarianism" (further developed in Frankfurt 2015). Even John Rawls, arguably the most influential political philosopher of the twentieth century, and known for his theory of (distributive) justice, in which he argues that rising inequality is only fair if the worst off in society benefit most (1971, 1993),[10] writes, in one of his important later works (*Political Liberalism*), that comparing conditions should be avoided:

> [G]iven our assumption throughout that everyone has the capacity to be a normal cooperating member of society, we say that when the principles of justice (with their index of primary goods) are

satisfied, none of these *variations among citizens* are unfair and give rise to injustice .... Justice as fairness rejects the idea of *comparing* and maximizing overall well-being in matters of political justice. (1993, pp. 184–188, emphasis added)

This implies a focus on alleviating people from absolute poverty, rather than from relative poverty, that is, economic inequality. The difference is depicted in Figure 5.4. In situation 1 and 2, the emphasis is on the increase of relative poverty – the difference between 1 and 2 is the direction of income or wealth development of the poor – whereas, in situation 3, the only relevant question is whether the poor are above the poverty threshold.

Some respond to this notion of absolute poverty by arguing that it is relative too. They often refer to the fact that poverty thresholds are socially constructed and change over time – poverty now is different from poverty in the late nineteenth century (Hall, 2014) – or that it varies over space: from country to country. However, this type of relativeness is quite different from relating a person's income position to others' within the *same* society at the *same* time:

[A]bsoluteness of needs is not the same as their fixity over time. The relative approach sees deprivation in terms of a person or household being able to achieve less than what others in that society do, and this relativeness is not to be confused with variation over time. (Sen, 1983, p. 155)

It is probably best to say that the absolute poverty level is contextual. This does not, in any way, diminish the moral relevance of focusing on

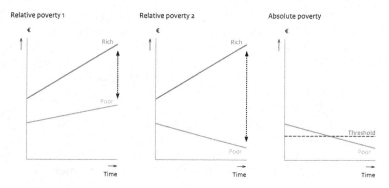

Figure 5.4 Relative and absolute poverty compared.

poverty *thresholds*. Sen even argues that focusing on inequality may obscure our sight on poverty. If there is a decline in prosperity because of a recession or depression, leading to great misery, starvation and hardship among a large part of the population, inequality statistics may not pick up on that since the relative picture – let us say the ratio between the top and bottom 10% (see Chapter 3) – need not change or even indicate a lower level of inequality (Sen, 1983, pp. 156–157). This is exactly what Piketty illustrates when he writes about his home country, France:

> [I]t is striking to see the extent to which the compression of income inequality is concentrated in one highly distinctive period: 1914–1945 …. To a large extent, it was the chaos of war, with its attendant, economic and political shocks, that reduced inequality in the twentieth century. (2014, p. 275; also cited in Atkinson 2015, p. 55)

Thus, in this time period, greater equality coincided with great poverty. Put to the extreme, there may be great inequality with everyone above the poverty threshold and great equality with everyone below it.

Although measuring equal shares is much easier than determining when someone has enough according to their needs, this is not a moral reason to neglect the doctrine of sufficiency and protect the doctrine of egalitarianism, argues Frankfurt (1987, p. 24). A perfectly measured equal share may fall short in fulfilling a person's needs.

Social primary goods

But, the question remains, enough of what, poverty of what? What is it that people should not be deprived of? John Rawls finds the answer in what he calls 'social primary goods'. In *A Theory of Justice* from 1971 and *Political Liberalism* from 1993, he advances the idea of 'justice as fairness,' using the two principles mentioned before, and with the outline of a list – an 'index' of 'social primary goods' – that everyone should possess or have access to, as free and equal persons:

a)   basic rights and liberties …;
b)   freedom of movement and choice of occupation against a background of diverse opportunities;
c)   powers and prerogatives of offices and positions of responsibility in the political and economic institutions of the basic structure;

d) income and wealth; and finally,
e) the social bases of self-respect. (Rawls, 1993, p. 181)

Rawls derives the notion of primary goods and this specific list (while admitting that other goods may be added, and that it needs to be specified in constitutional and legislative stages) from a hypothetical 'original position' (1993, pp. 304–310), in which people, as 'rationally autonomous representatives of citizens in society', as Rawls would have it, deliberate on the terms of 'fair social cooperation'. These people are assumed to be rational (i.e. they pursue the ends for themselves and those they represent) and, at the same time, reasonable (i.e. they, in Rawls's words, 'desire a social world in which they, as free and equal, can cooperate with others on terms all accept'). In other words, 'the reasonable society is neither a society of saints nor a society of the self-centred' (1993, p. 54). In addition, these people's social positions, native endowments, and historical accidents are to be put behind a 'veil of ignorance' (1993, pp. 23, 79). Those should be ignored, as they may unjustly affect the conception of what is 'right'. Rawls states that such a list of primary goods is what people, 'however distinct their content and their related religious and philosophical doctrines,' will perceive as right as long as they were to decide on that list in 'the original position' (1993, p. 181). Income and wealth (primary good 'd' in Rawls's list) are the material 'all-purpose means' that people need to make effective use of their liberties and rights. As argued before, Rawls seems to take an absolutist view on income and wealth, as he is concerned with the wealth and income of the least advantaged in society, and less with the relative differences: 'whatever the level of those inequalities, whether great or small' (1993, p. 6).[11]

The moral relevance of (economic) segregation

The moral relevance of economic inequality has been debated quite extensively in the literature. To our knowledge, this has not yet been done specifically for (economic) segregation. Similar to inequality, segregation is a relative concept as well, since it refers to the extent to which high- or low-income groups are more or less present in some neighbourhoods than other groups: 'residential (economic) segregation is the degree to which two or more (wealth or income) groups live separately from one another, in different parts of the urban environment' (Massey & Denton, 1988, p. 282, parentheses added; see also Chapter 3, Tammaru, Marcińczak, van Ham, & Musterd, 2016, p. 17 for a similar definition). Is the fact that the rich and the poor live (increasingly) apart from one another of moral importance in and of itself? Again, we look at it intrinsically here, and not instrumentally, which has been the focus in regard to the neighbourhood effects discussion in Chapter 4.

In line with the 'doctrine of sufficiency', the same reasoning applies as for economic inequality: it is more important that you have enough material resources than that others (in other neighbourhoods) have more (Sen, 1983; Frankfurt, 1987; Moroni 2013, 2015). The fact that people live physically separated does not alter this moral claim. However, there is a second element to this. It may be the case that, in one or several neighbourhoods, the level of basic facilities and amenities is below a threshold of what we generally consider socially acceptable. This is what we may call a 'slum' (e.g. Jacobs, 1961) – nowadays, the term seems to be reserved more for the informal settlements in developing countries – or a deprived neighbourhood. One could say that a slum or a deprived neighbourhood is a neighbourhood with a large number of people deprived of wealth and/or which is itself deprived of basic conditions.

A 'slum', like poverty, is an absolute concept, not a relative one. A neighbourhood is a slum or not; we do not say it is 'slummier' or 'less slummy' than another. Once a neighbourhood shifts below a particular culturally and politically determined prosperity threshold, it becomes a slum. This may justify policies to 'unslum' it and push it back above the threshold. In *The Death and Life of Great American Cities*, Jane Jacobs (1961), too, seems to take an absolutist position, as she is concerned with slums, slumming and unslumming, and much less with segregation and desegregation. The fact that slum thresholds vary over space and time, as it does in the case of (absolute) poverty, is irrelevant and does not take away from the idea that having a threshold, rather than a (relative) comparison between neighbourhoods, is absolutist (Sen, 1983). Therefore, Jacobs also rejects the idea of levelling differences between neighbourhoods through largescale social-mixing schemes and forced relocation of the slum population in exchange for middle-class outsiders; this is what she calls 'slum clearing'. This reduces economic segregation in a city but does not necessarily improve the living conditions of the original slum population. Genuine 'unslumming of slums', she argues, occurs through the 'advancement and self-diversification in a population' (Jacobs, 1961, p. 285). Yet again, the focus is on the prosperity of poor people and poor neighbourhoods, rather than on what other people and other neighbourhoods possess.

What may such facilities that determine whether a neighbourhood becomes a slum or stays out of that danger zone be? Moroni (1997, as cited in Basta 2016) transfers the idea of Rawls's primary goods to space by defining spatial 'primary goods' that people would agree on, again 'in the original position' and under a 'veil of ignorance'. Moroni distinguishes between four spatial primary goods: decent housing, access to basic transport, availability of green areas and a safe living environment. This is the very minimum people should have access to in their neighbourhood. The index of spatial primary goods is by no means fixed[12], nor is it, *a priori*, clear what the different goods comprise (for instance, what do 'safe,' 'decent,' and 'basic' entail exactly?). These are implementation issues that have to be determined in a political process, as they are inevitably contextual.

Thinking in terms of access to spatial primary goods also sheds a different light on the topical issue of 'gentrification' (see also Chapter 2), of which unslumming is a specific form. Many who emphasise the negative side of gentrification focus on the fact that some people can no longer afford to live in neighbourhoods that they, or, more generally, people of their wealth or income group, were able to reside previously (Atkinson, 2004). However, if affordability of homes in all neighbourhoods for all people from every income group were to be the moral focus, then we must conclude that there are very few neighbourhoods in developed cities (if any) where *everyone* could afford to live. And, conversely, there are many neighbourhoods in modern-day cities that are only affordable for very few people within society. Many people, also from middle- and higher-income groups, cannot afford to live in parts of London, such as The City, Chelsea and Kensington, within the *Périphérique* of Paris, in Manhattan and large parts of Brooklyn and Queens in New York, and in Amsterdam's canal area (the *Grachtengordel*). To create housing affordability for everyone in every neighbourhood seems practically unfeasible and, from a sufficiency standpoint, its moral relevance questionable.

From an absolutist view on poverty, it is morally unjust to allow some people to live with insufficient (spatial) means. In line with the idea of sufficiency, which rejects absolute poverty, and the necessary presence of and access to spatial primary goods, the moral focus should be on decent housing for all (wherever that is, and whatever the threshold of *decent*) and spatial access to jobs. In practice, this means that city regions or, more generally, daily urban systems must be able to accommodate people from all income or wealth groups. This is quite different from the option, or even the right, for everyone from any wealth group to be able to live *everywhere* in the city or city region, an implicit moral ideal in a lot of the critical neighbourhood-gentrification studies.

Then, cities should guarantee that these spatial primary goods are provided and accessible, which does not mean they need to be provided publicly; provision may occur privately or through contractual communities (Webster & Lai, 2003; Webster, 2007). In addition, cities or national governments should remove access barriers as much as possible, since there may be 'institutional' constraints to the access of primary goods, such as a housing system's inability to provide affordable housing for everyone.

Reflecting on the material dimension of *economic* inequality and segregation

Debates around *economic* inequality and (absolute) poverty have a material focus as they are concerned with resources, commodities (primary) goods (see section 'The same or enough? About the moral relevance of economic inequality') or consumption options (see Chapter 3). In other words, they are concerned with money. That is, however, a narrow indicator for standard of living. According to Sen, commodity ownership or availability is not the right focus for expressing someone's standard of living (1983, p. 160). So-called 'resource-based approaches' provide little answers to the fundamental question: 'what are people actually able to do and to be?' (Nussbaum, 2011, pp. 20, 59). Sen argues that the *capability approach* is a 'serious departure from concentration on the *means* of living to the *actual opportunities*' (2009, p. 233).[13]

A capability needs to be sharply distinguished from a *commodity* and its *characteristics*, but also from its *utility*, or the mental reaction to a functioning. Sen (1983, p. 160) takes the example of a bike. A bike is a commodity, a good. A bike's characteristic is that it can be set in motion and be made to transport someone. Then someone needs the capability to ride it – to get on it, to move the peddles, to be able to brake, to stay in the lane, and not to fall off. Riding a bike from one place to another may give utility, happiness, satisfaction or pleasure. The bike, or any good, is in and of itself not a good proxy of the standard of living, says Sen, because, when you are disabled, for instance, a bike is of little use. Nor is utility, which concentrates on the mental reaction to the use of the bike.[14] Not riding the bike because I am not able to, and sitting at an outdoor café instead, may make me equally happy or even happier. That is, however, not the point. The ability to ride the bike and having the choice to do so, or to refrain from doing so, is what reflects the standard of living according to Sen and many followers, and not the bike itself or the joy of riding it. For Rawls, income level (i.e. the size of primary *goods*) is sufficient to identify in what state people find themselves (1993, p. 366).[15]

What are those capabilities?

The recognition of capabilities as an indicator for standard of living has led to the development of the capability approach by Sen (2009), Nussbaum (2011), and many others.[16] Sen (2009) refuses to compose a universal and definitive list, as he argues that different contexts and cultures lead to different selections of valuable capabilities (Robeyns, 2005, p. 105; Chiappero-Martinetti & Moroni, 2007, pp. 370–371). Nussbaum is more specific in this regard and identifies ten capabilities (see box).

Absolute capability poverty

The capability approach is concerned with a minimum and absolute capability *threshold* for each of the ten capabilities, above which everyone should be able to find themselves (Wolff, 2007; Nussbaum, 2011, pp. 24, 36). In other words, capability improvement is determined in relation to an absolute norm, and not in terms of the distance toward the capabilities of others within society (i.e. capability inequality). However, the exact definition and measurement of the threshold are contextual again: every country has its own traditions, cultures, and norms. Developed countries usually apply a higher threshold than developing countries (are able to) do. This relativeness is not to be confused with the relativeness of *comparing* capabilities. Here, too, the way capability poverty comes about is contingent upon one's circumstances and social networks and may depend – in the event neighbourhood effects are present (see Chapter 4, section 'The negative impact of economic segregation') – on the neighbourhood (Chiappero-Martinetti & Moroni, 2007, pp. 370–371).[17]

Nussbaum's ten capabilities

1 Life (being able to live a normal life and not die prematurely);
2 Bodily health (being able to have good health);
3 Bodily integrity (being able to move freely and without being violated);
4 Senses, imagination and thought (being able to use the senses, to imagine, think and reason);
5 Emotions (being able to feel attachments to things and people);
6 Practical reason (being able to form a conception of the good);
7 Affiliation (being able to connect to and care for other people);
8 Other species (being able to live with others);
9 Play (being able to laugh and play);
10 Control over one's environment (political and material).

Segregation and capabilities

As the emergence and development of capability deprivation are contingent, people's capabilities are a function not only of personal factors (e.g. physical condition, skills), but also of social factors (e.g. social norms, power relations, networks) and environmental factors (e.g. climate, geographic location) (Robeyns, 2005, p. 98). Some of the social and environmental factors are established at the neighbourhood level. Segregation may lead, especially if it persists over generations, to spatial poverty traps (Grant, 2010), not just in the material sense, but in terms of capabilities. People may lack positive role models and may be negatively affected by cultures of unemployment, crime and misery. However, Chapter 4 already questioned the presence of sizeable neighbourhood effects on economic positions and chances.

The capability approach received attention in the urban planning literature as well (e.g. Davoudi & Brooks, 2014; Basta, 2016). Basta (2016) has made the approach spatial or urban, as she discusses capabilities in relation to the 'spatial primary goods' (Moroni, 1997) that we discussed earlier. The availability and accessibility of decent housing, basic transport, green areas and a safe living environment are necessary but not sufficient conditions in order to live a meaningful life. Not everyone possesses the capabilities to use these goods in such a way that brings them above a state of deprivation. For instance, someone may lack the capabilities for prudent bookkeeping and saving enough money for the rent. There may be a role for public (urban) policy here (see Chapter 6).

Notes

1   This chapter owes much to the work and thinking of Stefano Moroni (especially Moroni 2013, 2015; Chiappero-Martinetti and Moroni 2007), although the usual disclaimer applies.
2   These are the better known alternatives to egalitarian justice. Discussions of other forms such as communitarian, feminist and Marxist justice can be found elsewhere (e.g. Harvey 1972; Smith 1994, pp. 86–115).
3   See http://www.tradingeconomics.com/united-states/gdp for more information on this.
4   Stiglitz (2012) points to the exception of monopolistic rent-seeking behavior, which is behavior of individuals or organisations, such as banks, that use their monopoly position to extract money from others. According to Stiglitz, that behavior often leads to a *negative*-sum game.
5   Opportunities are never fully equal due to unequal talents. True or full equality of opportunity is elusive as it must 'involve special remedial treatments, or perhaps even, eventually, genetic engineering. But that seems to make equality of opportunity identical with equality of outcome' (Radcliffe-Richards, 1997, p. 254).

6 Arneson (1989, p. 91) identifies one divergence from Sen's approach, but we consider that marginal and beyond the scope of this book.

7 This is a distinction made by, for instance, Dworkin (1981b, p. 293) and Cohen (1989, p. 908).

8 For Dworkin (1981a, 1981b), the objection to subsidising expensive tastes is as strong in the case of genetic predisposition as it is when it results from deliberate and voluntary choice (see also Wolff, 2007).

9 It needs to be noted that we use these arguments to show the practical problems in achieving equality and nonsegregation. This does not make Nozick's political conception of justice right in and of itself. In his 'entitlement theory of justice,' Nozick rejects the idea of 'end-state principles' of justice, such as egalitarian justice, and, instead, considers a distribution just if the original *acquisition* of holdings and the *transfer* of holdings take place by legitimate means. Legitimate is acquisition and transfer without stealing, fraud, enslavement, preventing others from living freely and without excluding others from exchanges (1974, pp. 150–153). In other words, his emphasis is on the way the distribution has come about rather than the distribution itself. According to Rawls, there are various problems with this. One is that Nozick is not concerned with how just the initial distribution or basic social structure was or has come about. When one starts trading from an unjust starting point, such as not everyone possessing basic 'social primary goods' (see section 'The currency of equality of opportunity'), every individual voluntary transaction may be just, but the structure itself and the final distribution ceases to be just (Rawls, 1993, p. 266).

10 This is his second principle of justice, referred to as the 'difference principle': 'social and economic inequalities are [...] to be to the greatest benefit of the least advantaged members of society' (Rawls, 1993, p. 6). We mentioned the first before: 'each person is to have an equal right to the most extensive basic liberty compatible with a similar liberty for others' (Rawls, 1971, p. 60).

11 We say 'seems' since Rawls's position on the relative-absolute poverty dimension is not entirely clear. Rawls's 'difference principle' prescribes: 'social and economic inequalities are ... to be to the greatest benefit of the least advantaged members of society' (1993, p. 6). But, from that phrase, we cannot make out if those least advantaged members are (absolutely) poor; it is a statement about relative poverty. At the same time, he is not concerned with the level of inequality (main text above) and rejects 'comparing ... overall well-being in matters of political justice' (1993, p. 188).

12 One may want to add good schools and health care for instance.

13 'The distinction between achieved functionings and capabilities is between the realized and the effectively possible' (Robeyns, 2005, p. 95).

14 Utility has been the focus of utilitarianist views of justice (think, for instance, of Jeremy Bentham and John Stuart Mill). The greatest utility for all was deemed to fulfil the criterion of justice. This was criticised by Rawls and replaced by the notion of 'social primary goods,' which was then criticised and supplemented by the capability approach (Robeyns, 2005; Nussbaum, 2011).

15 Rawls responds in the following way: 'I have assumed throughout, and shall continue to assume, that while citizens do not have equal capacities, they do have, at least to the essential minimum degree, the moral, intellectual, and physical capacities that enable them to be fully cooperating

members of society over a complete life. Recall that for us the fundamental question of political philosophy is how to specify the fair terms of cooperation among persons so conceived .... I agree with Sen that basic capabilities are of first importance and the use of primary goods is always to be assessed in the light of the assumptions about those capabilities' (1993, p. 183). Variations in preferences and tastes are variations above the threshold of basic capabilities and irrelevant from the point of view of political philosophy; if people have expensive tastes, that is their own responsibility (Rawls, 1993, p. 185).

16 There has been critique on the capability approach (see Robeyns, 2005 for an overview). According to Hartley (2009), for instance, identifying and scoring capabilities does not challenge the roots of social injustice and the dominant power relations.

17 We agree with Chiappero-Martinetti & Moroni (2007, pp. 372–373), who say that the absolute conception of capabilities that Sen and Nussbaum defend at an *ethical* level – in other words, their moral focus - is perfectly compatible with a relativist position at an *explicative* level – in other words, absolute capability deprivation may be *caused* by differences in, for instance, the strength of social networks and the proximity of role models.

References

Arneson, R. J. (1989). Equality and equal opportunity for welfare. *Philosophical Studies, 56*(1), 77–93.

Atkinson, R. (2004). The evidence on the impact of gentrification: New lessons for the urban renaissance? *European Journal of Housing Policy, 4*(1), 107–131.

Atkinson, A. B. (2015). *Inequality – What Can Be Done?* Cambridge, MA: Harvard University Press.

Basta, C. (2016). From justice in planning toward planning for justice: A capability approach. *Planning Theory, 15*(2), 190–212.

Chiappero-Martinetti, E., & Moroni, S. (2007). An analytical framework for conceptualizing poverty and re-examining the capability approach. *The Journal of Socio-Economics, 36*(3), 360–375.

Cohen, G. A. (1989). On the currency of egalitarian justice. *Ethics, 99*(4), 906–944.

Corak, M. (2013). Income inequality, equality of opportunity, and intergenerational mobility. *Journal of Economic Perspectives, 27*(3), 79–102.

Davoudi, S., & Brooks, E. (2014). When does unequal become unfair? Judging claims of environmental justice. *Environment and Planning A, 46*(11), 2686–2702.

De Vos, M. (2015). Ongelijk maar fair. Waarom onze samenleving ongelijker is dan we vrezen, maar rechtvaardiger dan we hopen [Unequal but fair. Why our society is more unequal than we fear, but more fair than we hope for]. Tielt, the Netherlands: Uitgeverij LannooCampus.

Dorling, D. (2010). *Injustice: Why Social Inequality Persists*. Bristol, UK: The Policy Press.

Dorling, D. (2014). *Inequality and the 1%*. London, UK: Verso.

Dworkin, R. (1981a). What is inequality? Part I: Equality of welfare. *Philosophy and Public Affairs, 10*(3), 185–246.

Dworkin, R. (1981b). What is inequality? Part II: Equality of resources. *Philosophy and Public Affairs, 10*(4), 283–345.

Frankfurt, H. (1987). Equality as a moral ideal. *Ethics, 98*(1), 21–43.

Frankfurt, H. (2015). *On Inequality*. Princeton, NJ: Princeton University Press.

Grant, U. (2010). Spatial inequality and urban poverty traps. ODI/CPRC Working Paper Series No. WP326 (ODI), No. WP166 (CPRC). Overseas Development Institute, https://www.odi.org/sites/odi.org.uk/files/odi-assets/publications-opinion-files/5502.pdf

Hall, P. 2014. *Cities of Tomorrow: An Intellectual History of Urban Planning and Design Since 1880*. Oxford, UK: Wiley-Blackwell.

Hartley, D. (2009). Critiquing capabilities: The distractions of a beguiling concept. *Critical Social Policy, 29*(2), 261–273.

Harvey, D. (1972, reprinted in 2009). *Social Justice and the City*. Athens, GA: The University Press.

Hayek, F. A. (1944). *The Road to Serfdom: Text and Documents—The Definitive Edition. The Collected Works of F. A. Hayek* (Vol. 2). Chicago, IL: University of Chicago Press.

Jacobs, J. (1961). *The Death and Life of Great American Cities*. New York, NY: Random House.

Martin, R., Pike, A., Tyler, P., & Gardiner, B. (2015). *Spatially Rebalancing the UK Economy: The Need for a New Policy Model*. London, UK: RSA.

Massey, D. S., & Denton, N. A. (1988). Dimensions of segregation. *Social Forces, 67*(2), 281–315.

McCloskey, D. N. (2014). Measured, unmeasured, mismeasured, and unjustified pessimism: A review essay of Thomas Piketty's Capital in the twenty-first century. *Erasmus Journal of Philosophy and Economics, 7*(2), 73–115.

Miller, D. (1997). Equality and justice. *Ratio, 34*(6), 222–236.

Moretti, E. (2012). *The New Geography of Jobs*. Boston, MA: Houghton Mifflin Harcourt.

Moroni, S. (1997). *Etica e Territorio*. Milan, Italy: Ethics and Territory.

Moroni, S. (2013). *The responsible city. Institutional change and civic rebirth*. Rome, Italy: Carocci Editore.

Moroni, S. (2015, October). Absolute poverty, material inequality and the just city. Paper presented at a workshop on Urban Inequality and Justice. Utrecht, the Netherlands.

Nozick, R. (1974). *Anarchy, State and Utopia*. New York, NY: Basic Books.

Nussbaum, M. (2011). *Creating Capabilities: The Human Development Approach*. Cambridge, MA: Belknap Press.

Piketty, T. (2014). *Capital in the Twenty-First Century*. Cambridge, MA: Harvard University Press.

Radcliffe-Richards, J. (1997). Equality of opportunity. *Ratio, 10*(3), 253–279.

Rawls, J. (1971). *A Theory of Justice*. Cambridge, MA: Harvard University Press.

Rawls, J. (1993). *Political Liberalism*. New York, NY: Columbia University Press.

Robeyns, I. (2005). The capability approach: A theoretical survey. *Journal of Human Development*, 6(1), 93–114.

Sen, A. (1983). Poor, relatively speaking. *Oxford Economic Papers*, 35(2), 153–169.

Sen, A. (2009). *The Idea of Justice*. Cambridge, MA: Harvard University Press.

Smith, D. M. (1994). *Geography and Social Justice*. Oxford, UK: Blackwell.

Stiglitz, J. E. (2012). *The Price of Inequality: How Today's Divided Society Endangers Our Future*. New York, NY: W. W. Norton & Company.

Tammaru, T., Marcińczak, S., van Ham, M., & Musterd, S. (Eds.). (2016). *Socio-Economic Segregation in European Capital Cities*. London, UK: Routledge.

Thissen, M., de Graaff, T., & van Oort, F. G. (2016). Competitive network positions in trade and structural economic growth: A geographically weighted regression analysis for European regions. *Papers in Regional Science*, 95(1), 159–180.

van Ham, M., Hedman, L., Manley, D., Coulter, R., & Östh, J. (2014). Intergenerational transmission of neighbourhood poverty: An analysis of neighbourhood histories of individuals. *Transactions of the Institute of British Geographers*, 39(3), 402–417.

Webster, C. (2007). Property rights, public space and urban design. *Town Planning Review*, 78(1), 81–101.

Webster, C., & Lai, L. W. C. (2003). *Property Rights, Planning and Markets: Managing Spontaneous Cities*. London: Edward Elgar Publishing.

Wilkinson, R., & Pickett, K. (2009). *The Spirit Level: Why Equality Is Better for Everyone*. London, UK: Penguin Books.

Wolff, J. (2007). Equality: The recent history of an idea. *Journal of Moral Philosophy*, 4(1), 125–136.

6　Reflecting on urban policy

> Consider, for example, the orthodox planning reaction to a district called North End in Boston. ... it is officially considered Boston's worst slum and civic shame. ... In orthodox planning terms, everything conceivable is presumably wrong with the North End.
>
> (Jacobs, 1961, pp. 8–9).

The aim of our book is to reflect on the claim that 'urban-economic inequality and segregation are increasing, that this is a bad thing, and that money and people (in the case of segregation) need to be redistributed in response'. The first part has been dealt with in Chapters 2 to 5, and the next section summarises this. The question that remains is what the implications of these reflections could be for public policy in general, and urban policy in particular. We intend to shed light (see sections 'Redistribution of money' and 'Redistribution of people,' respectively) on common policy responses to the redistribution of *money* – through taxes, subsidies and so on – and *people* – through the social mixing of neighbourhoods and displacement of lower-income households.

Summary of the book

Chapter 2 describes the coming about of economic inequality and segregation in cities. We started off by saying that people differ in their possession of, and access to, material resources because they differ in human capital, and because people make different choices with regard to, for instance, household formation, education or jobs. However, currently, human differences are amplified by macro processes, such as globalisation, technological advancement and innovation. These processes put great emphasis on human capital. Highly trained and skilled workers benefit most, leading to income differences between these workers and those with fewer or other skills. This translates into differences *between* and *within* cities. In modern economies, the clustering of human capital (in cities) is pivotal, as it allows for benefitting from matching, sharing, and learning between people and businesses. Cities that are able to create and maintain such agglomeration effects outperform those that cannot. This may lead to an economic divergence between urban areas, as we perhaps see most pronounced in the United States. However, there are also processes of divergence and polarisation within cities. Until recently, cities were the main culmination points of deprivation. Due to the rise of the knowledge economy, which increased the importance of agglomeration effects, highly educated and highly paid workers move to or stay (after college) in cities, creating a duality of poor and rich within the city. This duality has a spatial-physical component as well – economic segregation. People of different income groups are not evenly distributed over cities as a result of their residential preferences and options. Economic inequality is, as such, a necessary condition for economic segregation. That said, the way and the degree in which segregation occurs is contextual – it depends on a country's and city's welfare, housing and spatial rules and practices.

In Chapter 3, we demonstrate that research choices with regard to the different measures and different elements of the economic or spatial distribution can influence the conclusions about (changes in) economic inequality and segregation in cities to a large extent. In the case of economic inequality, for instance, it is important to keep in mind that the available measures differ in their sensitivity to different parts of the economic distribution. While, for instance, values of the Gini coefficient may suggest that income inequality among inhabitants of a city is limited, other measures may pick up that significant income differences still exist between the extremes of the income distribution. Findings about inequality also depend on which economic *indicator* is used. High levels of wage inequality, for instance, may still be accompanied by lower differences in consumption options, as individuals may possess different levels of savings. Thus, for a good understanding of economic inequality and segregation in practice, using multiple measures and indicators, which produce different complementary results, is necessary to provide an accurate picture (Massey & Denton, 1988, p. 283). However, providing such a snapshot of the level of economic inequality and segregation in one or multiple years is not *sufficient*, we believe. It does not tell us much about the dynamics of people within the income or wealth distribution and the spatial translation thereof. This is important, though, to assess if people do improve their lower-income position or neighbourhood at some point (Jäntti & Jenkins, 2015). In addition, it helps to analyse if slum neighbourhoods are capable of 'unslumming' or must be qualified as 'perpetual slums' (Jacobs, 1961).

When, and under which circumstances, are economic inequality and segregation in cities problematic? What are the negative effects and how substantial are those? In Chapter 4, we show that there is a clear danger of overattributing all sorts of negative social phenomena to urban-economic inequality and segregation. There are logical and empirical difficulties in doing so. The logical difficulty lies in the problem of causally identifying if, and to what extent, people behave according to whether others have more or less wealth. And, consequently, whether countries have more social and health problems because they have more significant income differences, or because of other factors, such as unhealthy diets. The difficulty in answering such a question unreservedly may be the key reason why empirical research shows ambiguous findings. In the case of segregation, too, there is much debate in the literature about the logical and empirical problems with identifying neighbourhood effects, and isolating them from selection effects (e.g. Cheshire, 2008; van Ham & Manley, 2012). Put more simply: are people poor because of the neighbourhood they live in, or does being poor affect where they live? This is not to say there are no negative effects – a lot more (advanced) empirical research needs to be done on this – but we simply argue that the evidence for the negative effects of economic inequality and segregation is rather bleak in comparison to the alarmism with which the two are being rejected in academic and political arenas. Perhaps the strongest case can be made for the social-psychological effects that occur because of the status anxiety that results from large and increasing wealth differences and spatial separation. But – relevant to this chapter on policy – does a mental reaction to a social phenomenon constitute a legitimate criterion for policy action? Those who answer this question with 'yes' should be aware of the fact that this opens the door to all sorts of policies that may improve social happiness and well-being for some/many people at the expense of the rights of others. This is a common critique, more generally, on utilitarianism, as discussed in Chapter 5.

In Chapter 5, we deal with the claim that economic inequality and segregation may be immoral in and of themselves. To those who claim this, economic equality and desegregation are 'just' and moral ideals worth aspiring to. In Chapter 5, in the section 'Equality and distributive justice,' we explain that, morally, 'egalitarian justice' may be questioned from the point of view of alternative principles of justice. In fact, we have tried to scrutinise the entire idea of *distributive* justice and *distribution* (of wealth and of location) by making explicit that the implicit notion of something or someone cutting and distributing an *a priori* fixed metaphorical pie is flawed. Also, we distinguished between different types of economic inequality, such as 'good' and 'bad' inequality; the latter being unequal economic outcomes as a result of inequality of *opportunities*. In addition, there are two groups of concerns about aiming for material equality and desegregation. The first is practical. How to strive for material equality while, at the same time, maintaining liberty and equal rights? For instance, if people get property rights over goods and the right to trade them, it is unlikely that during the process of trading a distributive pattern such as perfect equality emerges. In order to obtain that, liberty would have to be limited and equality of rights would have to be abandoned or suspended. The second concern does not deal with the practicability of striving for patterns, such as economic equality and desegregation, but with the moral relevance of such relative concepts *per se*. Here, we introduced Frankfurt's 'doctrine of sufficiency,' in which the moral concern is whether everyone has *enough* rather than the *same* (1987). And, finally, we reflected on the *material* focus in debates on economic inequality and segregation, and argue that we should not lose sight of the importance of *capabilities* and be aware of what people are able 'to do and be' (Nussbaum, 2011, p. 20).

Redistribution of money

We will deal with the issue of wealth distribution rather briefly for two reasons. The first is practical: our book needs to be compact, and many before us have already discussed this issue extensively, and probably with more authority than we could ever do (e.g. Stiglitz, 2012; Piketty, 2014; Atkinson, 2015). The second reason is substantive in nature. This book is about cities and, therefore, about *urban* policy. Regardless of the growing importance of cities (Glaeser 2011) and of local administrations (Barber 2015), wealth redistribution is likely to remain a policy affair that stretches beyond the city level to that of the nation state. This is not simply an empirical observation or expectation for the future; it is a matter of logic. In his book *City Limits*, Paul Peterson (1981) argues that cities have rather porous boundaries for capital and labour from other cities and the countryside, due to which city politics have to operate within the bandwidth of national or federal allocative policies.

As the (negative) effects of (urban-)economic inequality are not uncontested from an empirical and logical point of view (see Chapter 4, section 'The negative impact of economic inequality'), and as the notion that the moral relevance and desirability of economic equality can be questioned (see Chapter 5), questions may also be raised about policies that have reducing or eliminating economic inequality as their target. Is that desirable? A negative answer to that question obviously does not imply advocating policies that do *increase* inequality; it *only* asks the question whether relative poverty is a meaningful or important policy problem that needs targeting. In many cases, as we have seen in Chapters 4 and 5, it is not so much the *difference* in wealth that creates personal or social problems or immoral situations, it is people's absolute wealth *level* that is at the root of these issues.

This is not to say that particular income-generating (and inequality-enhancing) behaviour, such as monopolistic rent-seeking (see, references to Stiglitz, 2012, in Chapters 2 and 5), cannot be a valid moral concern. Think of excessive salaries to particular groups, such as bankers and some CEOs. Most people seem to be concerned with high salaries to these groups particularly, as those seem to be earned at the expense of the income of others, and less with the salaries to other rich people such as innovators and sportsmen. Consequently, they seem to care less about the *outcome*, and the inequality of it, but more about the morality of the (monopolistic rent-seeking) *behaviour* that leads to that outcome. That then questions the appropriateness of general redistributive measures. Or, as Deirdre McCloskey (2014) argues: 'if on ethical grounds we don't like high CEO salaries, why not legislate against them directly, using some more targeted tool than a massive intrusion into the economy?'

Reducing poverty and creating equal opportunities

Targeting absolute rather than relative poverty is not to say that redistribution is not needed. Redistribution may be necessary to obtain the required resources for reducing or eliminating absolute poverty. However, in the case of eradicating absolute poverty, redistribution of wealth is a means to an end, not an end in itself, as is the case with reducing relative poverty. In the case of the former, recouped wealth is used to improve the position of the poor, not to make the richer part of the income distribution worse off. In fact, in the light of discussions on economic inequality, alleviating poverty is no regret: it helps the poor and, as a byproduct, reduces economic inequality.

Do note, however, that redistribution of wealth is insufficient. Eliminating elitism, discrimination and unequal opportunities in general is not served 'simply' by a shift of wealth from one part to another part of the wealth distribution. Redistribution does not target fundamental inequalities in the treatment and *opportunities* of people; it only covers them under a thin layer of money (de Vos, 2015; Chapter 4). Those inequalities need to be eradicated, first and foremost, by the legal system, which needs to create *de jure* equal rights for everyone, if not yet present. But, equally important, and at the same time much more difficult (de, Vos 2015), is making sure that *de facto* people have equal rights, in other words, opportunities. This is not solely a governmental task – equality of opportunities is something that needs to be enforced and reproduced by society at large. It could, for instance, mean that access to a university should not rely on parental wealth, let alone on personal, biological characteristics, such as sex and race. Selection procedures at schools and universities should be explicitly and actively discriminatory on the grounds of talent, and non-discriminatory on all other grounds.

In the (ideal) case of equal opportunities, the inequality of material outcomes is the result of differences in talent and choices. But, even then, avoiding (absolute) poverty remains an important moral ideal.

Redistribution of people

'What is a city, but the people?' is a famous quote from Shakespeare's *The Tragedy of Coriolanus*. As with most rhetorical questions, the answer to the question is enclosed: 'The people are the city'. When people are 'redistributed' – relocated or displaced (involuntarily) through urban public policy aimed at social mixing – does it help them or the places they are displaced from? The literature distinguishes between people-based and place-based policies (Winnick, 1966; Bolton, 1992; Glaeser, 2011). While in practice we often see examples of place-based policies, many contributions to the literature prioritise people-based policies (e.g. Glaeser, 2011; Manville, 2012). However, empirically, we do see that poor people live concentrated in particular (poor) places (see Chapters 2 and 3). What could the policy implication of that observation be? Does it not also call for the inevitability of place-based policies?

Since economic segregation often goes hand in hand with economic inequality, the presence of poor neighbourhoods is one of the most visible examples of the presence of economic inequality in a city. Although economic segregation can have some advantages as well, the possible negative effects of economic segregation are the main reason that it is often considered as socially problematic. However, the additional effect of economic segregation is generally considered small (if present at all). This has some important implications with regard to policies that are aimed at creating mixed neighbourhoods based on the idea that this lowers (or eliminates) the presence of negative neighbourhood effects. Paul Cheshire goes as far as to state that mixed neighbourhood policies are 'belief-based policies' and that 'forcing neighbourhoods to be mixed in social and economic terms is ... mainly treating the symptoms of inequalities rather than the causes' (2008, p. 30). As a result, many urban-renewal policies aimed at social mixing, gentrification and replacing lower-income households with middle-income households can be considered ineffective, or sometimes even detrimental, in improving the displaced people's socioeconomic position (Miltenburg & van de Werfhorst 2017) or their neighbourhood satisfaction (Posthumus, Bolt, & van Kempen, 2014, pp. 25–28). Moreover, already in the 1960s, American sociologist Herbert Gans (1961) explained that a certain degree of homogeneity of neighbourhoods, in terms of class, race and age, allows people to build robust social networks that help them further in life. Consequently, along the lines of logic, reducing economic segregation and creating greater neighbourhood heterogeneity, along economic lines, is unlikely to reduce economic inequality.

Social mixing may primarily improve only the neighbourhood – the place – but even this could be questioned, as one may think differently about what improvement means. Property values, the tax base and governmental control over a neighbourhood are likely to increase, but social cohesion and involvement are found to decline (Gans. 1961; Atkinson. 2004; Bolt, Philips, & van Kempen, 2010; Gans, 1961; Uitermark, Duyvendak, & Kleinhans, et al. 2007; Bolt et al., 2010). In other words, even if neighbourhood poverty and livability are the policy targets, such policies often do not live up to (all) their expectations.

Improving the lives of poor people, rather than moving them around, seems ethically sound and practically more effective – at least, if people, not places, are the focus. Or, as Atkinson phrases it: 'it is perhaps sad that approaches to housing renewal and urban policy in this context are not being thought through in a more holistic way in order to encompass rather than displace lower-income households' (2004, p. 125). Alternatively, the primary focus should be directly on eradicating poverty and improving people's wealth and *capabilities* above a socially-defined threshold. While detailing of polices is beyond the scope of this book, as it is largely context-dependent, clearly education plays a vital role in capability formation.

Spatial primary goods

The focus on people rather than places does not mean there is no room or need for place-based policies. If some social problems are spatially concentrated, it may be most efficient to focus the policy on the inhabitants of that particular territory only, rather than to make it place-independent. This could be called *place-specific* people-based policy.

In addition, room also remains for what are commonly understood as place-based policies, namely *physical* (place-based) policies that change the spatial structure of neighbourhoods. In Chapter 5, we introuce the notion of 'spatial primary goods' (Moroni, 1997; Basta, 2016), a specific form of social primary goods that each individual should at least possess or have access to. One could think of decent housing, access to basic transport, availability of green areas and a safe living environment (Moroni, 1997; Basta, 2016). Their exact number, definition and actual operationalisation remain a contextual matter. At least, urban design must play a role in creating access to primary goods: 'some forms, such as low-density sprawl, pose a significant barrier when it comes to the provision of neighborhood-level facilities or access to jobs and urban services' (Talen, 2013, p. 130).

That said, creating spatial preconditions through urban design is unlikely to be enough. As argued before, possession of, or access to, spatial primary goods is only helpful if people possess the basic *capabilities* to use them (Basta, 2016). Developing these capabilities alongside the provision of spatial primary goods for poor people, especially those in persistently poor neighbourhoods ('perpetual slums', in Jacob's terms), seems a crucial cornerstone for an urgent and challenging urban-policy agenda.

References

Atkinson, R. (2004). The evidence on the impact of gentrification: New lessons for the urban renaissance? *European Journal of Housing Policy*, *4*(1), 107–131.

Atkinson, A. B. (2015). *Inequality – What Can Be Done?* Cambridge, MA: Harvard University Press.

Barber, B. (2015). *If Mayors Ruled the World: Dysfunctional Nations, Rising Cities*. New Haven, CT: Yale University Press.

Basta, C. (2016). From justice in planning toward planning for justice: A capability approach. *Planning Theory*, *15*(2), 190–212.

Bolt, G., Philips, D., & van Kempen, R. (2010). Housing policy, (de)segregation and social mixing. *Housing Studies*, *25*(2), 129–135.

Bolton, R. (1992). "Place prosperity vs people prosperity" revisited: An old issue with a new angle. *Urban Studies*, *29*(2), 185–203.

Cheshire, P. (2008, May). Policies for mixed communities: Faith-based displacement activity? Paper presented at the ESRC workshop on Gentrification and Social Mix, Kings College, London, UK.

de Vos, M. (2015). Ongelijk maar fair. Waarom onze samenleving ongelijker is dan we vrezen, maar rechtvaardiger dan we hopen [Unequal but fair. Why our society is more unequal than we fear, but more fair than we hope for]. Tielt, the Netherlands: Uitgeverij LannooCampus.

Frankfurt, H. (1987). Equality as a moral ideal. *Ethics*, *98*(1), 21–43.

Gans, H. (1961). The balanced community. Homogeneity or heterogeneity in residential areas. *Journal of the American Institute of Planners, 27*(3), 176–184.

Glaeser, E. L. (2011). *The Triumph of the City: How Our Greatest Invention Makes Us Richer, Smarter, Greener, Healthier and Happier.* New York, NY: Penguin.

Jacobs, J. (1961). *The Death and Life of Great American Cities.* New York, NY: Random House.

Jäntti, M., & Jenkins, S. P. (2015). Income mobility. In A. Atkinson and T. Bourguignon (Eds.), *Handbook of Income Distribution* (Vol. 2A, pp. 807–935). Amsterdam, the Netherlands: Springer.

Manville, M. (2012). People, race and place: American support for person- and place-based urban policy, 1973–2008. *Urban Studies, 49*(14), 3101–3119.

Massey, D. S., & Denton, N. A. (1988). The dimensions of residential segregation. *Social Forces, 67*(2), 281–315.

McCloskey, D. N. (2014). Measured, unmeasured, mismeasured, and unjustified pessimism: A review essay of Thomas Piketty's *Capital in the Twenty-First Century. Erasmus Journal for Philosophy and Economics, 7*(2), 73–115.

Miltenburg, E. M., & van de Werfhorst, H. G. (2017). Finding a job: The role of the neighbourhood for different household configurations over the life course. *European Sociological Review, 33*(1), 30–45.

Moroni, S. (1997). *Etica e Territorio* [Ethics and Territory]. Milan: FrancoAngeli.

Nussbaum, M. (2011). *Creating Capabilities: The Human Development Approach.* Cambridge, MA: Belknap Press.

Peterson, P. (1981). *City Limits.* Chicago, IL: The University of Chicago Press.

Piketty, T. (2014). *Capital in the Twenty-First Century.* Cambridge, MA: Harvard University Press.

Posthumus, H., Bolt, G., & van Kempen R. (2014). Victims or victors? The effects of forced relocations on housing satisfaction in Dutch cities. *Journal of Urban Affairs, 36*(1), 13–31.

Stiglitz, J. E. (2012). *The Price of Inequality: How Today's Divided Society Endangers Our Future.* New York, NY: W. W. Norton & Company.

Talen, E. (2013). Urban in/justice. In C. Basta & S. Moroni (Eds.), *Ethics, Design and Planning of the Built Environment* (pp. 125–132). Dordrecht, the Netherlands: Springer.

Uitermark, J., Duyvendak, J. W., & Kleinhans, R. (2007). Gentrification as a governmental strategy: Social control and social cohesion in Hoogvliet, Rotterdam. *Urban Studies, 39*(1), 125–141.

van Ham, M., & Manley, D. (2012). Neighbourhood effects research at a crossroad. Ten challenges for future research. *Environment and Planning A, 44*(12), 2787–2793.

Winnick, L. (1966). Place prosperity vs. people prosperity: Welfare considerations in the geographic redistribution of economic activity. In *Essays in Urban Land Economics* (pp. 273–283). Los Angeles, CA: Real Estate Research Program.

Glossary

Absolute poverty Refers to a state of affairs in which someone is considered poor because their level of wealth is below an absolute (politically, culturally or otherwise determined) threshold.

Capital The balance between a person's financial and material possessions and their debts.

Distributive justice The principle of moral rightness regarding a distribution (of wealth, for instance). There are various principles of rightness under this heading, such as egalitarian justice, utilitarian justice, justice as fairness, and the entitlement theory of justice.

Economic inequality A state in which not everyone has the same income or wealth, leading to a skewed distribution of income or wealth.

Egalitarian justice A specific principle of distributive justice in which a distribution is considered right if everyone has (more or less) the same.

Entitlement theory of justice A specific principle of distributive justice, as developed by Robert Nozick, in which a distribution is considered right if it came about the right way; that is, through the voluntary and nonfraudulent acquisition and transfer of holdings.

Gentrification It refers to the process of economic 'upgrading' of relatively poor urban areas (usually neighbourhoods), primarily through the inflow of people with more wealth than the existing and previous population.

Income The income of an individual or household is the sum of all earnings someone received over a certain period of time.

Income inequality A state in which not everyone has the same income, leading to a skewed income distribution.

Justice The principle of moral rightness.

Justice as fairness A specific principle of distributive justice, as developed by John Rawls, in which a distribution is considered right if it is 'to the greatest benefit of the least advantaged members of society' (Rawls, *Political Liberalism,* 1993, p. 6; see Chapter 5).

Neighbourhood effect   An effect that occurs if there is an *additional* (positive or negative) effect of neighbourhood characteristics on individual outcomes.

Polarisation   A process in which the high end and the low end of the labour market or the income distribution are increasing in absolute terms or relative to the middle class.

Relative poverty   Refers to a standard of living in which someone is considered poor(er) because they have less wealth than someone else.

Segregation (urban economic)   '[R]esidential (economic) segregation is the degree to which two or more (wealth) groups live separately from one another, in different parts of the urban environment'. (Massey and Denton, 'The dimensions of residential segregation' 1988, p. 282, parentheses added; see Chapter 3).

Selection effect   The possibility that the mechanisms (e.g., unemployment or low income) that 'select' people in specific neighbourhoods (expensive, i.e., 'good,' or cheap, i.e., 'deprived' neighbourhoods) are not independent from the outcome studied (e.g., estimating the chance that someone is unemployed based on the level of deprivation of neighbourhoods).

Urban economic inequality   A skewed income or wealth distribution within the context of a city or city region.

Utilitarian justice   A specific principle of distributive justice in which a distribution is considered right if it leads to 'the greatest good for the greatest number'.

Wage   Income derived from employment.

Wealth   *See Capital.*

Index